THE ENGLISH DOG AT HOME

FELICITY WIGAN
WITH VICTORIA MATHER

Photographs by GEOFFREY SHAKERLEY

CHATTO & WINDUS
LONDON

HALF TITLE: *HRH the Princess Anne's dogs Random and Apollo in the hall of Gatcombe Park.*

FRONTISPIECE: *Chutney at home.*

TITLE PAGE: *Cuthbert Montagu relaxing in Scotland.*

First published in 1986
by Chatto & Windus Ltd
40 William IV Street
London WC2N 4DF

British Library Cataloguing in Publication Data

Wigan, Felicity
The English dog at home.
1. Dogs—Anecdotes, facetiae, satire, etc.
I. Title   II. Mather, Victoria
636.7'00207   SF426.2

ISBN 0 7011 3121 7

Designed by Behram Kapadia

Colour origination by Waterden Reproductions

Photoset by Rowland Phototypesetting Ltd,
Bury St Edmunds,
Suffolk
Printed by
Roundwood Press,
Warwick

CONTENTS

To Chutney

FOREWORD

THE cushions were plumped, not a crease to be seen; the fire flickered, not a log out of place; parrot tulips, forced lilac and lilies covered the table in profusion. The photographer's assistant studied the light meter for the twentieth time and the photographer sighed with relief: perfection at last.

At the crucial moment a Great Dane ambled into the room, carefully picked his way through the camera leads and flashing lights, settled comfortably on the sofa and closed his eyes.

The photographer stared in amazement, his face contorted with fury.

Chutney had made his point. This was his home, his room and his sofa.

To me, the onlooker, the photograph – intended to be of the room itself – had come to life. Chutney had demonstrated that the English interior is not complete without the dog, the most precious member of so many English families.

An idea born in my mind that moment became reality a few months later thanks to the support and encouragement of Geoffrey Shakerley, who must be the greatest dog-loving photographer. Dogs and their owners alike fell for his charm, patience and wonderful sense of humour. Although we decided not to impose Chutney on our readers, his loyalty and comfort during hours of toil with my tape-recorder and notes were invaluable. A cold nose and a huge paw were thrust into my face at frustrating moments. These became more and more frequent until finally I found myself unable to cope alone.

Victoria Mather, friend and saviour, came to my rescue, and I would like to thank her for unfailing support, for the hours of deciphering my illegible scrawl, correcting my appalling grammar and above all restoring my confidence in a comparatively short working schedule. Without her help I am convinced that the writing would have been finished in the year 2000.

I am grateful to Jan Dalley, our editor at Chatto and Windus for her advice and guidance and to Jane Moores whose transcription of the many tapes were essential and beautifully executed under great pressure.

Geoffrey Shakerley has made this book possible, marvellous fun to do, and I would not have survived with any other photographer.

Finally, my thanks and love to my extremely long suffering family and certain friends, two-legged, four-legged and feathered who supported me throughout eight months of canine chaos.

FELICITY WIGAN

Felicity tells me that Chutney gave her the idea for this book. I can believe anything of this remarkable dog but, if he will forgive me, I must also put on record the extent of Felicity's own contribution. Her enthusiasm throughout has made the compilation of this book a work of pure pleasure. Her spontaneous affection for all dogs and her infectious personality have immediately made all our subjects feel at ease, whether confronted by the camera or tape-recorder.

For me she was invaluable: warming hands that had become so cold on a Kent beach they could no longer operate the camera, carrying heavy equipment and setting up lights, arranging rooms to their best advantage, and above all providing inspiration when inventiveness flagged.

My debt to her is incalculable.

Together we are of course greatly indebted to our canine stars.

Any actor will tell you that it is fatal to act with animals. I can only add that the same is true of photography. The antics we had to employ to attract attention would have made us the envy of any circus clown. Innumerable bags of dog biscuits were consumed in our attempts to obviate a natural stubbornness.

Notwithstanding, we have emerged bowed but unbloody. Not a bite – not even so much as a growl were we accorded during the long sessions with our stars. Surely a fine tribute to their temperament and co-operation.

Our final debt of gratitude is to all the owners. Their willingness to be involved, their patience over the unaccustomed length of the photographic sessions and their continued support have made our task a happy and painless one. Above all, their unbounded generosity has meant that in all our travels we have never had to stay in any hotel.

This is now their story – one of companionship and care, loyalty and love, and a rare community of spirit.

GEOFFREY SHAKERLEY

Lambchop

SIR TATTON SYKES, BART

SLEDMERE is an Edwardian – Georgian house, rebuilt as a perfect replica of the original house destroyed by fire in 1911.

Lambchop is a bull terrier, a breed which combines the original gladiatorial qualities of the bulldog with the talents of the terriers. Lambchop has lived at Sledmere in the Yorkshire Wolds for thirteen years, during which time she has enslaved the master of the house, Sir Tatton Sykes, the butler and the plumber.

Bull terriers are never slender, but at one point Lambchop swelled to the sense of occasion at Sledmere to such an extent that she weighed four stone. Even slimline, Lambchop is a slow mover. She slinks, which is the most dignified way of doing things deliberately. During the monthly concert in the library at Sledmere, Lambchop may be seen slinking silently down the grand staircase. Pausing briefly for breath by the splendid statue of the Apollo Belvedere (a 1780 copy by Wilton, of which the original is in the Vatican), Lambchop cocks an ear to Beethoven and, having deduced that the guests are unlikely to be dispensing chocolate biscuits in her direction, decides the party is not for her. Lambchop's expression implies long and complicated thought processes, all of which are concentrated on food. Having dismissed the concert, she ambles towards the more reliable option of the kitchen. She takes another breather in the Horse Room, below a painting of Sir Tatton Sykes (4th baronet) with Sir Tatton Sykes (stallion). The man was an ornament of

ABOVE: *Lambchop surveying the work of Capability Brown.*

LEFT: *The grand staircase at Sledmere – Lambchop and Tatton discuss the concert in progress in the library above.*

sporting England and attended 74 St Legers, a race which the horse won in 1846; in the same year J. F. Herring Senior painted the picture of them both. It was this Sir Tatton who built up the Sledmere Stud to be the largest in England with 320 head of stock. Horses bred at Sledmere have won the Derby, the Oaks, the Two Thousand Guineas and the St Leger.

After her refreshing contemplation of these triumphs Lambchop continues towards the larder, only pausing to give the Turkish Room a desultory glance.

The Turkish Room is a maverick First World War introduction to the otherwise classical house. It was designed for Sir Mark Sykes, the present Sir Tatton's grandfather, who was an eminent Orientalist and an extensive traveller in the Middle East during his younger days. The knowledge he acquired then was put to good use by the British Government during the 1914–18 war, when Sir Mark was employed on tricky negotiations in Egypt, Arabia and Syria, drawing up the Sykes-Picot Agreement in 1916. He then had the bad luck to die of influenza, aged thirty-nine, while attending the Peace Conference in Paris in 1919.

It was an Armenian artist, David Ohanessian, who fulfilled Sir Mark's whim to reproduce in his North Yorkshire home one of the Sultan's apartments in the Valideh Mosque in Istanbul. The tiles were made in Damascus under the supervision of Ohanessian, who later designed the street signs still to be seen in Jerusalem.

Sadly, the Turkish Room was not completed, and never fulfilled its potential as a Turkish bath. The cold water plumbing was installed, but never the hot. Sir Tatton says, 'My surviving aunts well remember the horrors of being thrown into the icy pool by their father'. The pool in question has now been replaced by the gentleman's lavatory. Nor were the decorations finished, as one of the boats carrying the tiles from Turkey was sunk during the war. Sir Tatton is planning to bathe the existing ceramics in light.

Sir Tatton succeeded his father, Sir Richard Sykes, in 1978 at the age of 35. He has since implemented a continuous schedule of improvements to Sledmere, including planning a complete eighteenth-century orangery over the Italian Garden. It was a Richard Sykes from Hull who, having inherited an old manor house on the same site through the female line, originally began to transform it into a classical oeuvre; he laid the first stone of the new Sledmere on 17 June, 1751. But it was his grandson, Christopher, who continued the design on an even grander scale, for when he took possession of the property in 1776 he promptly engaged Capability Brown to plan the layout of the two thousand acre park. This included demolishing the old village and re-building it out of sight of the house, the same humble exercise Brown carried out for the Duke of Devonshire at Chatsworth.

In the early 1780s Sir Christopher engaged architects John Carr and, later, Samuel Wyatt, to make improvements and additions to the 1751 design which included turning the whole house round so that the main front faced south.

In 1789 Sir Christopher was introduced to Joseph Rose, the most famous English plasterer of his day, a favourite of Adam and Wyatt and a Yorkshireman, the latter his most distinguished characteristic in his new patron's eyes. Rose designed and executed all the decorative plasterwork at Sledmere and also played a major role in the completion of the interior,

Lambchop daydreams as Tatton works in his newly converted sitting room on the first floor of Sledmere.

ordering furniture, upholstery and wallpapers. When the fire in 1911 destroyed everything except the four outer walls, the dairy and the laundry, the drawings for Joseph Rose's plasterwork were saved from the library and used, in conjunction with Rose's original moulds, by architect Walter Brierley (who had inherited Carr's practice in York) in the exact reconstruction of the house.

From family accounts of the fire Tatton recalls 'wretched stories about a horse-drawn fire engine struggling to Sledmere from Malton, which is about twelve miles away, then being quite unable to cope because of its pathetic little water cart. It was a slow, strong fire and went on for about

BELOW: *Aunt Angela's mural in the former schoolroom now appropriated by Tatton for his private dining room – a small gathering of pigs on the table are part of a large collection belonging to Tatton.*

three days, so all the contents of the house were removed except four pieces of Chippendale furniture and two carpets, one of which matched the ceiling of the drawing room, the other the ceiling of the library.'

Today the library is as monumental and magnificent as originally intended by Sir Christopher Sykes. Architectural historian John Cornforth has written that 'It is as if the recollections of the Baths of Caracalla and Diocletian have been combined with those of the Renaissance galleries of the Palazzo Farnese and Villa Madama looking out over the formal gardens, but here terrace and fountains are replaced by the amphitheatre of Brown's landscape. Few great Georgian interiors and views are so closely integrated, and the whole concept suggests the controlling hand of a knowledgeable and independent-minded amateur.'

It is in another amateur family production that Lambchop comes into her own. In the former schoolroom, now appropriated by Tatton for his private dining room, a curious mural relieves the heavy panelling. Painted by Tatton's Aunt Angela, Countess of Antrim, it is a conversation piece featuring fantasy (a German schloss) and reality (Lambchop squatting on a balustrade). The little castle in the centre was designed, possibly by Capability Brown, to be the estate offices at Sledmere. The schloss, reminiscent of one of mad King Ludwig's efforts, is balanced on the opposite side of the picture by the seat of the earls of Antrim, Glenarm Castle in County Antrim. Aunt Angela has also thrown in for good measure the Mussenden Temple, which was built by the Earl Bishop of Derry in the eighteenth century and now belongs to the National Trust. (Later, as Marquess of Bristol, the Earl Bishop went on to greater extravagances at Ickworth, near Bury St Edmunds in Suffolk.) Centre stage in this theatrical work Marie, the Sykes's nurse, is pushing the family's future heroin addict, Uncle Daniel, in a pram, followed by a self-portrait of the artist as a little girl. Behind them Lambchop's father, Bullseye, chases butterflies. It was an occupation to which he was devoted. Stage left lurks Mademoiselle Fanny Ludovicy, the family's governess from

Luxembourg, known as Mouselle. 'She was here at the beginning of this century teaching my grandfather's children how to be good Catholics,' says Tatton. 'But not very successfully. My father was the worst Catholic imaginable and so must Uncle Daniel have been, with all his heroin shooting, lipstick, powder and paint.' Mouselle gave up the unequal task when Sir Richard succeeded and became the family's keeper of cast-off greyhounds, two of which feature alongside Lambchop in the picture. Their elegance only serves to emphasise that this was Lambchop in her heavyweight days, before a stringent diet reduced her post-natal figure problem.

Lambchop has had two litters of puppies, but motherhood did not suit the lady. She murdered her first-born quite deliberately.

'She only allowed one puppy to survive as a crippled monster which now lives in the village,' recalls Tatton with a shudder. 'She was a perfectly brutal mother, which was shattering – I had had to whelp the first litter and it was one of the most dreadful experiences of my life.'

'It was only surpassed in horror by the experience of mating her a second time. The Chop went to a splendid, tough woman from New Zealand who lived near Harewood to be united with a tri-colour bull terrier. He was a brute of a dog and much to my chagrin I was made to take part in the marriage ceremony. Mrs Ewart firmly told me to pick up a mat and follow her and we disappeared into what can only be described as a bunker. I was told to get down on my knees and she got down on her knees and we both held our dogs and for the next forty minutes spun round on those mats in the awful concrete bunker trying to get the dogs to do what they were supposed to do. My dog really hates sex and the whole business was quite hysterical.'

The result was six beautiful puppies. 'They had wonderful, huge wrinkly skin six sizes too big, inside which was a person – all professionally whelped to thwart Lambchop's homicidal inclinations. 'Otherwise Lambchop has been perfectly charming all her life, wonderful with human beings and particularly good with children,' says Tatton. 'There was only one occasion when I found myself carrying her by her back legs with a Jack Russell in her mouth. Bull terriers' jaws lock and they will not let go, so you need a pepper grinder. If you grind pepper over the dog's face they let go sharpish. But who has a pepper grinder in their pocket all day long?'

The bull terrier was bred as a fighter during the last century when dog-fighting was still (just) legal, and considerable sums of money were wagered on the chances of the new nimbler, pugnacious breed. It also enjoyed a reputation as a ratter and keeper of low company, but won literary fame in Charles Dickens' *Oliver Twist* as Bullseye, the bull terrier belonging to Bill Sykes (no relation). In 1860 a Birmingham breeder, James Hinks, produced the first pure white strain, which achieved success among the pedigree dogs on the show benches. This did not seem to impair the fighting qualities of the breed.

The British Encyclopedia of Dogs may say that the bull terrier's 'particular shape attracts only a limited number of fanciers' but, if so, Sir Tatton Sykes is one of a rare breed. 'I shall go on having bull terriers at Sledmere for ever and ever. They will all be the same rare red colour, I hope, and they will all be called Lambchop.'

16

Lambchop, mistress of the house, awaiting guests in the hall at Sledmere.

Cuthbert

MRS DRU MONTAGU

As the clock struck eleven, a cross between a wire-haired clothes brush and a caterpillar slithered down the stairs. Cuthbert was executing his levée.

He is the scion of a distinguished line. Dandie Dinmonts are one of the older breeds of terrier which first appeared around 1700 in the Scottish borders and was christened by Sir Walter Scott in his romance *Guy Mannering*. On his travels Scott is said to have met a Mr James Davidson of Hawick who owned some of these dogs; Scott was so beguiled by the breed, with their soulful eyes yet fierce skill hunting badgers, otters and foxes, that he made Mr Davidson the hero of his novel under the guise of sporting farmer Dandie Dinmont and his game little terriers. When the book was published in 1814 the breed, which became very popular, was named after Dandie Dinmont.

A letter of James Davidson's records that his dogs were 'Tarr, reddish and wire-haired, a bitch; Pepper, shaggy and light, from Dr Brown, of Borjenwood. The race of Dandies are all bred from the two last.' It is rare to know the actual names of the two dogs from which the official standard breed is descended. The earlier Dandies of the eighteenth century probably evolved from rough native border terriers. Today the breed remains rather exclusive, as enthusiasts prefer to keep the numbers small so that the Dandie's original characteristics will not deteriorate.

Cuthbert lives in London, Wiltshire and Scotland, but naturally his Scottish home is his favourite because he can pursue his traditional sports

ABOVE: *The somnolent posture is deceptive.*

LEFT: *Cuthbert and Minnie at home in Scotland.*

of investigating foxes' earths and getting stuck down rabbit holes, from which he has had to be retrieved by the root of the tail.

After such busy country days, Cuthbert enjoys languorous nights on the bed of his mistress, Minnie Montagu. 'He always sleeps on his back, exposing his three-piece suite. Imagine, he was a rather dull, unattractive puppy and it actually took me a year to fall totally in love with him. I fell in love with his eyes and that huge black nose, I adore his big fat paws. Divine, naughty Cuth, you are so beautiful!' Cuthbert's soulful eyes imply that Minnie has been beating him all day long.

Actually he has been denied a shooting expedition with Minnie's husband, Dru, who shares Minnie's passion for Cuthbert with rather less enthusiasm. 'He's a nightmare out shooting,' she says. 'He longs to grab the birds – he can kill them by shaking them – so he sits and howls instead.' At the mention of shooting one ear goes up – 'He understands every word I say' – and Cuthbert yawns, revealing the special birthmark on his tongue. 'It looks like a tealeaf. Poor Cuthy, I took a knife and tried to scrape it off; it's lucky he's *so* long-suffering. And particularly wonderful with the children. I once found them trying to stick a pair of scissors up his bottom, but all Cuthy did was stare resignedly down his long back. That was when I knew he would never, ever hurt them.'

Even fleas have failed to dull Minnie's love affair with Cuthy. 'It just makes me love him even more: I sit in the car watching fascinated as the fleas clamber over his back. In Scotland he's terribly dirty and dishevelled, which simply makes him even more wonderful.'

Cuthbert is an accomplished swimmer, habitué of sea and river, and an enthusiastic flyer. 'He trips on to aeroplanes and loves it because he knows he is coming up here. But he is so well-balanced nothing makes him nervous.' Cuthy also enjoys entertaining, supervising Minnie's preparations for shooting parties with minute attention to detail. The refectory table is swept clear of books, flowers and children's toys to be replaced with large baskets, lined in immaculate white linen, seething with lobsters. 'We live on lobster or langoustine. I can't cook when I'm trying to be nice to people so we have hundreds of lobsters instead,' says Minnie.

Cuthbert's Scottish home is a small glen farmhouse sitting squarely in a cottage garden brimming with flowers and vegetables. Green trellis softens the austere reddish walls, allegedly built from the stones of a castle which stood in the glen centuries before. Inside flowers bloom in china bowls and jugs throughout the house, and the flower motif is repeated in *petit point* on the tapestry fire screens and in the watercolour paintings. A mass of cushions and paisley shawls invite a tired dog to disguise himself on the heavy tweed sofas round the open fire. Just savouring the joys of rabbiting or a trip to the beach can be quite exhausting, even for a dog who never gets up before eleven o'clock. Asleep on the sofa with his top knot flattened, Cuthy resembles a grey, whiskery old tramp wearing a squashed top hat.

But the somnolent posture is deceptive. At the sound of a car in the drive the huge liquid brown eyes snap open and thirty pounds of pepper-coloured Dandie Dinmont hurtle to the floor in the hope of hearing his master's voice.

It is not Dru Montagu but another visitor. Though disappointed, Cuthbert is not a dog to miss an opportunity. The gate is open, so he can make his bid for freedom and rabbits, hopping and skipping like Mrs Tiggywinkle across the field towards the heathery purple hills.

Minnie gazes despairingly from the window. 'He'll go for hours now and I always think he's lost. I'll get quite hysterical and wait up for him, sometimes until one in the morning, then he comes back eventually all bedraggled and with totally raw feet so I haven't the heart to beat him. I just pet him and love him because I know he simply can't help himself when it comes to rabbits.'

Private moments.

Marcus and Brancus

Mrs John Loudon

TITLES as imposing as Shrover Symphonic Prince and Shrover Emperor Concerto should give a dog a good name. Better known as Marcus and Brancus, these aristocrats live at Tichborne Park, which has been in their mistress's family for more than eight hundred years.

The original house at Tichborne was in existence by 1293, and one Chidiock Tichborne, when about to be executed for his part in the Babington Plot in 1586, claimed his family were in Tichborne two centuries before the Norman Conquest in 1066. It obviously meant a great deal to him. However, strict documentary evidence shows that the Bishop of Winchester granted part of his Tichborne estate as a sub-manor for one Walter de Tichborne around 1135.

As the eldest Miss Tichborne, Anne Loudon inherited the present Georgian house which was built in 1803 in Tichborne Park. Thirteen years ago she was looking for one cocker spaniel puppy when brothers Marcus and Brancus persuaded her that they were both adorable and inseparable. Anne and her husband Johnny proved a pushover. From the beginning Marcus was convinced he was a person, while Brancus posed as an extremely fierce guard dog.

'Marcus wanted to live his life in my lap, on the drawing room sofas, the dining room chairs during meals and on our pillow at night,' says Anne. 'Brancus barked and snapped at the majority of people who dared to darken our doors – usually the men who had finally come to mend the washing machine, heating or burst pipes.'

ABOVE: *Marcus and Brancus with Anne Loudon beside the River Itchen at Tichborne Park.*

LEFT: *Trout spotting beside the moat in the garden behind the chapel wing.*

LEFT: *The spaniels with Anne under the family portraits in the drawing room at Tichborne.*

Nor do the spaniels have much respect for the conventional rules of hospitality. 'I remember arranging a very important and slightly pompous business dinner,' says Anne. 'The smoked salmon was all individually laid out on the dining room table and we were chatting politely over drinks. When I ushered the guests into the dining room Marcus was presiding over the empty plates on a chair at the end of the table, licking his chops. Brancus was standing guard on the floor by his side.'

The two brothers have a symbiotic relationship. When Brancus was run over in the village, rushed to the vet and returned home after intricate surgery on his leg, Anne and Johnny Loudon naturally lavished most of their attention on the invalid. Marcus instantly developed an agonising limp. Pronounced sound by the vet, he had come out in sympathy.

The chapel at Tichborne is part of the original thirteenth-century house and was reputedly the scene of one of Henry VIII's marriages. Marcus and Brancus attend Catholic mass with the family and it was at midnight mass one Christmas that, unseen, they shared Aunt Magda's pew in the gallery. Unseen, but not unheard. All was well until the bell rang for communion, to which Marcus and Brancus reacted by barking like mad. At Aunt Magda's vociferously whispered command of 'SIT!' the entire congregation obediently sat down.

Marcus and Brancus have indulged their hunting genes by taking a keen interest in the historical background of their home, spending many happy hours digging up the most cultivated and colourful parts of the garden in search of early ancestors and remains of Tichborne martyrs who failed to survive the Reformation.

They have assisted their mistress with the annual Tichborne Dole, a tradition instituted in the thirteenth century by Lady Mabella Tichborne. As she lay dying she asked her husband if he would grant her the means to leave a charitable bequest of a dole of bread for any poor folk applying to Tichborne House on Lady Day, 25 March. Sir Roger Tichborne, in his munificence, granted his dying wife corn for this dole from all the land she could walk round while a brand was burning. Too weak to walk, Lady Mabella succeeded in crawling round a twenty-three-acre field, still known as 'The Crawls' and where Marcus and Brancus have enjoyed some fine rabbiting.

Lady Mabella took out the insurance policy of laying a curse on any of her successors to discontinue the dole, the penalty being a generation of seven daughters, the demise of the family name and the collapse of the ancient house. When the dole was temporarily discontinued in 1796, because Dole Day had become somewhat dissolute and rowdy, part of the house fell down seven years later and the next baronet produced seven daughters. The dole was reinstated until the Second World War broke out. The name has now died out but the dole continues today in the form of a bag of flour distributed at Tichborne on Lady Day.

Now elderly gentlemen, the spaniels commute with Anne and Johnny between the country and London where, in Chelsea Square, they have discovered a new game of cocking their legs against starched nannies in the gardens.

RIGHT: *Awaiting lunch under the portrait of Anne Loudon's grandmother, Lady Tichborne – Marcus is notorious for occupying any vacant seat in the dining room.*

Mozart and Patty in the garden at Dummer Grange.

ABOVE RIGHT: *In the drawing room of Dummer.*

Mozart

MRS CHARLIE PALMER-TOMKINSON

MOZART enjoys a little Richard Strauss. A refreshing siesta to *Also Sprach Zarathustra* is an excellent digestive after three and a half pounds of offal. For Mozart is a St Bernard of vigorous appetites, stringent prejudices and torrid passions. He is the lord of the manor of Dummer Grange, a rambling red-brick Jacobean house with gabled wings nestling in a maze of yew hedges and tall flint walls. In five years he has established his authority over everyone.

His passion for fragrant, fresh loaves finally defeated the breadman. After merrily chasing the van up and down the drive for months, it all became too tempting for Mozart. He stowed away. Halfway to the village the breadman had that uncomfortable feeling that someone was staring at him. Someone was actually breathing heavily down the back of his neck. Someone was rather bored, having eaten his way through most of the loaves. After providing a daily service for many years the breadman has never again delivered to Dummer Grange.

Mozart owns Patty Palmer-Tomkinson, who has painstakingly jacked up everything in her kitchen, including the Aga, to a height above St Bernard level. Ladders to the larder have finally thwarted Mozart's prurient interest in human haute cuisine. Charlie Palmer-Tomkinson, reduced to a cypher in his own house, has generously devised a Mozart door-opener. By a pulley operated with Christmas ribbon he can now open the door for the dog while eating eggs and bacon at the breakfast table.

ABOVE: *A refreshing siesta in the master bedroom.*

Of all Mozart's passions his grandest is for Mr Feathers whose job is to decimate the pigeon population whenever increasing numbers threaten the crops. The cull completed, the pigeons are laid out on his cottage lawn. The perfect dog's dinner. But one day when the pigeons had been taken away to be plucked and Mr Feathers' own dogs were out to lunch elsewhere, Mozart's appetites were unleashed upon Mr Feathers, whom he subjected to amorous, but unrequited, attentions. It was an extremely irate pigeon shooter who returned the over-excited St Bernard.

'Poor Lulu,' says Patty. 'No-one over thirty likes him and people always leave this house walking backwards.' And clutching dry cleaning vouchers. The provision of a towel in every room in the house is proof of the continuous, loving dribble from Mozart's chops, which is merely an over-exuberant expression of his appreciation of visitors. His coat sheds hairs, so clothes brushes are issued to weekend guests on arrival, just as they have tripped over the giant tin in the hall labelled MOZART'S KIT, complete with horse-sized grooming brushes and flea powder.

When Mozart ambles into the drawing room to stalk unsuspecting guests they retreat, picking up handbags, clutching children, handy cushions and elderly aunts. Mozart skilfully negotiates the occasional table and introduces himself to each person eyeball to eyeball. His own eyes, deep set, dark, with drooping lower lids, are surrounded by a mass of wrinkles, like prunes set in spaghetti. Wide shoulders taper down a heavy, powerful body, covered in coarse-cut orange marmalade fur with a white tummy and a comical tail, that waves like the White Ensign.

Mozart's bosom friend is Hector the yellow Labrador. Whereas Mozart is a ponderous navigator, Hector barges his way into the legs and affections of strangers. The marmalade hearthrug and the yellow peril are bed and board companions: a double basket at night, jowl by bowl at feeding time. Once when Mozart's bowl was invaded by a hungry hedgehog, Hector was delegated by the St Bernard to remove the unattractive hors d'oeuvre.

A dog of discrimination, Mozart does not like rain or Hector going off shooting with his master. Mozart is decidedly bitter about being excluded from the gundogs' trade union. On shooting days he applies his enormous brain to flying picketing, spends a frustrating morning hunting the shoot, then exacts an exquisite revenge by lolloping among the assembled labradors and spaniels at the crucial moment when it is raining pheasants. He is banned by lunchtime.

Mozart is at his best in the snow, displaying a proper sense of history. His ancestors were heroes of the Alps, thought to have been originally bred in the twelfth century by monks belonging to the hospitaller community of St Bernard. Whether or not the dogs, with kegs of brandy attached to their collars, went to the aid of snowbound travellers is a matter of conjecture. A St Bernard, weighing up to two hundred pounds, is one of the heaviest and strongest dogs in the world.

Mozart has only spent one night away from home. Hitch-hiking on the A30, he was spotted by the local police who telephoned the Palmer-Tomkinsons to say a 'thin, bedraggled' St Bernard was loose on the road. 'Certainly not Mozart,' retorted Patty, the three and a half pounds of offal she had fed him for supper still vivid in her memory. Then she changed her mind. 'After all, how many St Bernards would be walking down the side of the A30 at four o'clock in the morning?' Luckily a kindly couple had already taken pity on this thin, bedraggled St Bernard and stopped. Mozart, thrilled at the thought of a lift in a nice warm car, hopped in. He had a wonderful night. Dried with a hairdryer, fortified with a reviving snack of lamb cutlets, sausages and steak, he sank into a contented slumber on the best guestroom brass bed.

Now his nocturnal activities are confined to home. Each summer evening Mozart and Hector retreat beneath the cherry tree at the top of the garden to survey their small world: the ducks and delphiniums, visitors returning home down the drive and the shadows lengthening from Dummer Grange's seventeenth-century chimneys.

BELOW: *Mozart's coat sheds regardless of regular tricology treatments – clothes brushes are standard issue to weekend guests.*

Archie, Tigger and Bandit

THE DUCHESS OF ROXBURGHE

'YOU are the sort of person who would pick your dog up in your arms but let your children run loose to be trampled by the crowd.' That was the accusation levelled at Lady Jane Grosvenor by a man expounding his anti-British views at Speakers' Corner in Hyde Park. Then unmarried and childless, she had indeed just clasped her whippet, Jamie, to her bosom to protect him from the milling throng, but today, as Duchess of Roxburghe, she is more likely to be carrying a puppy through a coach party of visitors come to see her husband's ancestral castle in Scotland.

The Duchess of Devonshire once said that Chatsworth was a terrible place in which to house-train a puppy. In the seventy-five rooms at Floors Castle, near Kelso in Scotland, there is also plenty of scope for little accidents to happen unnoticed. And when the castle is open to the public and certain doors locked, only two escape routes remain to green grass. 'You either have to go down some very dangerous wooden steps or through the main entrance,' says Janie Roxburghe. 'And if a coach party has arrived you have to struggle through the crowd with the puppy in your arms, and the puppy can't wait, so by the time you reach the lawn you are soaking wet but the puppy is happy.'

Janie has two whippets, Archie and Tigger, successors to Jamie who died last year at the aged of sixteen, and Bandit, a brindle lurcher who is the newest recruit to the Roxburghe ménage. Janie had always wanted a lurcher, hoping the breed would be more suited to Scottish country life

ABOVE: *Bandit asleep in the library.*

LEFT: *Archie, Tigger and Bandit with Janie in the hall at Floors Castle, under a painting by Hendrick Danckerts of Charles II and courtiers walking in Horseguards parade.*

ABOVE: *A morning ride with Janie gives the ideal excuse to chase hares.*

than the elegant but frail whippets. 'They get quite cold up here and badly torn on all the barbed wire. Their skin is so soft it tears like silk.' Whippets are sporting hounds, bred for speed, and the dogs run so fast that they skim under the fences, regardless of the danger. Jamie once had twenty-eight stitches after a piece of barbed wire became embedded in his back and, although Tigger was given his name because of the striped markings on his back, these have been obliterated by scars.

Despite their presence at Floors Castle, whippets are the only members of the greyhound group not to have been selected and bred along pure lines in aristocratic circles. The pharaohs and the czars may have kept sleek, sporting greyhound-like animals, but the whippet owes it origins to the mining communities where people wanted an inexpensive sport. The first recorded breeder was one John Hammond, at work between 1870 and 1880, and the whippet, small, friendly, easily housed and fed, offered the miners the opportunity to own and breed the dogs them-selves. They were originally called the 'snap-dog' by miners in the coalfields of north-east England because of their lightning acceleration in pursuit of rabbits. Keen gamblers raced whippets over 200 yards, making the breed the fastest in the world over short distances. Nor has their rabbiting prowess diminished. During the miners' strike of 1984–85 a good whippet was a prized procurer of free food for miners' kitchens.

And the Duke of Roxburghe recently received a stern letter from his game-keeper saying that his grouse moor would be greatly improved if Her Grace's dogs did not chase the hares.

The sturdier lurchers were bred to gypsy life, travelling at the heels of their master's horse. Every day, Bandit accompanies Janie Roxburghe as she rides through the rolling park that encompasses Floors. His gypsy heritage is close by. 'There is an old place in the hills called Kirk Yetholm,' Janie explains, 'which was the last place of the gypsy settlers. There used to be a gypsy king there, so it is very much lurcher country, and Kirk Yetholm was where one of Bandit's family came from. He was conceived during a gypsy gathering on St Boswell's Green.'

If their forebears were at home in a gypsy camp or a miners' cottage, the dogs make their presence felt in a castle. Their baskets hog the fire in the library, a room which still boasts many splendid volumes despite the sale of the famous Roxburghe library in 1812 to fund the lawsuit establishing Sir James Innes's right to the succession. At that sale a first edition of *The Decameron* fetched £2,260 and Caxton's *Recuyell of the Historyes of Troy* made a thousand guineas, both huge sums in those days.

Today the dogs' chocolate drops and Smarties sit among the leather-bound volumes. The Duchess allows them to loll on the sofas, a sybaritic habit forbidden by the Duke – but the dogs can hear him coming through the front door two rooms away and be back in their baskets before that door has shut.

It is in the dining room that Archie's and Tigger's manners leave a little to be desired. Janie recalls, 'When we had the first really big dinner party after we got married, the table was beautifully laid with white damask and I came floating down to dinner all dressed up. I put the dogs out but it was raining and Tigger came back into the house covered in mud, got up on to the dining room table and ate all the butter and toast. There were little paw marks all over the table.'

The whippets have instructed Bandit in the fine art of thievery. 'He is at it non-stop and being much taller than the others can stand up on his hind legs and reach. He very often enjoys platefuls of cold meat in the pantry,' says Janie. Tigger once stole a sirloin of beef from the royal grooms who were spending the night at Floors in their caravan after the Scottish Driving Trials. 'Tigger got into the caravan and was seen dragging this piece of meat away, and about half an hour later he came back with his stomach bulging, looking frightfully ill, and promptly went back into the caravan to see if there was any more.'

One edible family heirloom has so far evaded the thieves. Entering the hall at Floors Castle through the grand *porte cochère* designed by the architect W. H. Playfair, centre stage among the cartridge belts, fishing flies and bloodstock magazines on the hall table, one sees a cake preserved under glass. It was baked specially for Guy Roxburghe's twenty-first birthday in 1975 'by chefs J. Collingbourne & G. Hogsflesh'.

The building of Floors was begun in 1721 and the original design by William Adam, father of Robert, was for a plain Georgian country house. It was when the sixth Duke James was twenty-one that he summoned Playfair, the architect of many handsome buildings in Edinburgh including the Scottish National Gallery and Donaldson's Hospital. At Floors he was allowed to let his imagination run riot, with dramatic results. The roofscape is as exotic as Chambord or Longleat; the overall ground area of

BELOW: *Birdwatching from the ruins above the Tweed.*

the castle comprises 1.075 acres. During its more recent history, the film *Greystoke* was made here.

Archie, Tigger and Bandit faithfully follow the Duchess through state rooms hung with family portraits by Sir Henry Raeburn, Sir Godfrey Kneller, Sir Joshua Reynolds and John Hoppner. There is a Chippendale mahogany commode in the hall, and in the drawing room a magnificent set of seventeenth-century Brussels tapestries brought from the Long Island home of the American Duchess May, wife of the eighth Duke of Roxburghe. She redesigned the ballroom to accommodate the Gobelins tapestry from the Portières des Dieux series by Claude Audran the Younger and employed a local craftsman to embellish the panelling with carvings in the style of Grinling Gibbons.

In the gardens the dogs supervise the cultivation of Floors Castle's carnations. Several original varieties such as the pink Duchess of Roxburghe and the dark red Duke of Norfolk were propagated there. The walled garden produces all the flowers, fruit and vegetables for the castle, including asparagus, melons, grapes, peaches and nectarines.

At home in the castle the dogs know that the chef's forbearance is limited, but they have made diplomatic inroads with Nanny, who supervises the nursery containing the five-year-old Marquess of Bowmont, Lord Edward Innes Ker, aged two, and Lady Rosanagh, aged seven. Tigger is now granted an audience and biscuits, a considerable improvement on the time when Rosie was born and the whippets were overcome with jealousy. 'Archie used to go into the nursery every day and do a dump on the carpet, so he had to be banned because otherwise we thought Nanny would throw a real wobbler,' says Janie.

She is happily resigned to the dogs' naughtiness. If the Roxburghes sit down to dinner and the tantalising journey of the trolley, laden with delicacies, is watched by only two beady-eyed dogs, Janie knows it means trouble. Upstairs in the Duke and Duchess's bedroom Bandit is tucking into two books, Janie's clothes and a carcase stolen from the chef.

Bandit, Tigger and Archie with Janie: Floors and the River Tweed provide a fairytale backdrop.

FIELD MARSHAL THE EARL
DER OF TUNIS
91 – 1969
L IRISH GUARDS

Connor

The Irish Guards

LATEST IRISH GUARDS RECRUIT

Recruit CONCHOBAR (CONNOR) MAC NESSA is set to become the ninth Regimental Mascot of the Irish Guards.

On 17 Jan 1985 Irish Wolfhound CONNOR will be formally welcomed into the Regiment by Her Majesty Queen Elizabeth the Queen Mother at Clarence House.

Still too young and inexperienced, he now faces twelve months' training by Lance Sergeant Rutherford and CORMAC OF TARA, the current Mascot.

CORMAC has indicated that he wishes to hang up his collar and put up his paws after eight years service, but is dogmatic that he will not do so until CONNOR has successfully completed his basic training.

When fully grown CONNOR can expect to weigh 170 lbs and stand six foot on his hind legs. His main duty will be to lead Irish Guardsmen mounting duties at either Buckingham Palace or Windsor Castle and to appear at many other ceremonial and public occasions. He will certainly have a prodigious appetite and think nothing of putting away three pounds of meat at a sitting.

FOLLOWING this press release, Conchobar Mac Nessa was formally enrolled into the regular Army. It is customary for the regimental clerks to record the wolfhounds' doings, a task which is entirely unofficial and a

ABOVE: *Connor guarding the officers' tunics – his own red linen tunic was made to measure by the Irish Guards' tailor.*

LEFT: *Connor with Lance Sergeant Brian Rutherford at Wellington Barracks, in front of the statue of Field Marshal, the Earl Alexander of Tunis which stands outside the Guards Chapel.*

source of amusement and no little inventiveness. His attestation paper was completed with a little help from Lance Sergeant David Rutherford ('How many children are dependent on you?' Answer came there 'None') and Connor took his oath like any other recruit, giving his pawprint in lieu of signature. Having sworn 'honestly and faithfully to defend Her Majesty, her heirs and successors, in person, crown and dignity, against all enemies', the new recruit to the Irish Guards was fitted for his uniform. A grey sheepskin coat, presented by the citizens of Windsor, served for the winter months while a superb red linen tunic was made to measure by the Guards' tailor from cloth made specially and given by the Irish Linen Guild.

This dog's life is suitably grand for one named after the ancient and victorious King Connor who ruled in Ireland around the time of Christ. He is waited on hand and paw by his loyal handler Lance Sergeant Rutherford, his wife Sally and four-year-old daughter Katherine, whose home at Chelsea Barracks, London, Connor dignifies with his presence. Lance Sergeant Rutherford is skilled in the art of wolfhound puppy haute cuisine: a light breakfast of two pints of milk and a couple of eggs; a sustaining luncheon of two pounds of meat served with meal and more eggs; then, if the young Connor felt peckish in the early evening, a snack of three more pounds of meat, meal and added vitamins. At the age of two, Connor rather reluctantly gave up these feasts in favour of one meal a day consisting of a mere four pounds of meat, two pints of milk, biscuit and meal.

Connor's training in official duties was accelerated by the unexpected death of his predecessor, Cormac of Tara, with whom Connor had been going to work in tandem during his adolescence. Cormac was a tough act to follow, a showman who had declined a personal present from the Queen Mother with a disapproving sniff. It was recorded for posterity on the company conduct sheet that Cormac was guilty of 'Conduct to the prejudice of good order and military discipline contrary to section 69 of the Dog Act 1955 in that he at Pirbright on 17 Mar 77 failed to eat the sweets offered to him by Her Majesty Queen Elizabeth the Queen Mother', a churlish act witnessed by 'World Press and a parade of hundreds'. The punishment awarded was no sweets for one month and a two-day ban from the NAAFI. Neither of these deterred Cormac from contravening that same section 69 of the Dog Act 1955 'in that he at Horse Guards Parade on 16 May 81 tried to take a nip out of the Japanese High Commissioner'. The witness on this occasion was the Prime Minister, Mrs Margaret Thatcher, and the punishment dire: 'restricted visits to stud farm'.

Connor's first brush with royalty passed without any such sensational incidents. As a small puppy he was introduced to Queen Elizabeth the Queen Mother at Clarence House, as part of his initiation into his life's work as the mascot of the Irish Guards. His training school was Chelsea Barracks, where he learned to walk ceremonially and sit still during the martial performances of the Band of the Irish Guards. A shy music lover, Connor has been detected in that profound state of cerebration sometimes mistaken for slumber.

Connor made his debut on St Patrick's Day. Along with every soldier in the Irish Guards he received his shamrock from the Queen Mother, who tucked a large spray neatly to his silver collar.

Connor and Lance Sergeant Rutherford awaiting orders in the colonel's office.

This collar is engraved with the names of two of his predecessors, Fionn and Cormac, but the Irish Guards first acquired a mascot in August 1902 when the Irish Kennel Club decided to present them with an Irish wolfhound as a regimental pet. Accordingly, an Irish Guards Wolfhound competition was held at the Kennel Club show at Crystal Palace and from a parade of eight dogs Mrs Gerrard's Rajah of Kidnol was selected. It is recorded in the regimental history that 'the Hon Mervyn Wakefield MP and Quartermaster Fowles together with Sergeant Major Burt and a few non-commissioned officers attended and received the dog on behalf of the regiment.' Its name was promptly changed to Brian Boru.

Irish wolfhounds supposedly have magical gifts. Finn, hero of one Irish legend, had a wolfhound called Bran endowed with a deadly poisonous claw and an ability to tell the future. Like the Irish Guards, Finn owned a succession of wolfhounds; another dog was said to be multi-coloured, wore a gold chain and was able to produce gold and silver out of its mouth. Legend aside, wolfhounds were used to hunt wolf and elk.

Connor is eighth in the Irish Guards' illustrious line of wolfhounds, donated, as was Cormac of Tara, by top breeder Miss Margaret Harrison. All kitted out in the silver collar, Connor is the very model of a modern mascot wolfhound, impeccably mannered, feet at the regulation 30-degree angle, unmoved by common, unruly dogs in a crowd. At home with Lance Sergeant Rutherford he's a very spoilt family pet. 'He's the best I've ever seen with children,' says David Rutherford, which is a happy coincidence as much of Connor's working life is spent visiting schools and hospitals; he has been groomed to be a highlight of children's Christmas parties.

As his official duties began, so did Connor's report book. Cormac's recorded that 'He must show more respect for the regimental sergeant major and stop growling when being inspected. He has had a good year with the battalion, has a mature and professional attitude to his duties but does have a wicked sense of humour and is still apt to give unsuspecting Japanese tourists a quick nip.' He obviously got a taste for it after that little incident with the Japanese High Commissioner.

Connor himself has been inculcated with these cautionary tales and is as yet innocent of any such conduct unbecoming.

The mascot of the Irish Guards at home on duty in front of the parade ground at Wellington Barracks.

Sonia, Pinky, Muppet, Alexander, Toya, Buster, Figaro and Zola Budd

SIR JOHN WIGGIN, BART

HONINGTON Hall is the perfect English country house. Built during the seventeenth century, gracefully proportioned, secluded in a park with the river Stour flowing below the garden and the village church at the door. Three Bank Holiday visitors were admiring this dignified scene when an elderly man burst out of the bushes driving a tractor and followed by a flotilla of dachshunds and two white ferrets. Sir John Wiggin was taking his dogs for a walk.

Johnny Wiggin acquired his first dachshunds in Germany during the war. He found two pathetically thin puppies among the bomb damage in Wuppertal and put them in his scout car. 'My orderly, Guardsman Stanford brought them up by feeding them with a fountain pen filler for two months. I was going to call them Kraut and Sauerkraut but no fraternisation was allowed in 1944, so they ended up as Pork and Beans. They were the most popular dogs in occupied Germany.'

Pork and Beans returned to Honington with Sir John in 1947 and, after quarantine, became the first in the long line of dachshunds that have been at the hall ever since. Lady Wiggin remembers that, when she was first

ABOVE: *Who was the culprit?*

RIGHT: *The octagonal salon returned to former glory.*

ABOVE: *Honington Hall provides the classic winter backdrop to the Wiggin family.*

married, her husband kept seven dogs on their bed. 'I woke up thinking I'd had a stroke. I'd lost all feeling and couldn't move because all the bedclothes were pinned down tight by dachshunds.' The late Sherry-Boo acted as a sleeping draught. 'She got very old and smelly and her breath was pure anaesthetic. It sent us to sleep immediately, we've never slept as well since the Great Reaper took her,' says Sir John sadly.

The present complement of dachshunds consists of three maiden aunts, Sonia, Pinky and Muppet, their brother Alexander who married Toya ('Spratts did the catering for the wedding,' says Sir John) and produced Buster, Figaro and Zola Budd, so named because she ran fastest to the bottle.

The ferrets are also part of the family, although the Wiggins are still in mourning for Bryan, half ferret, half polecat, who kept the dogs in admirable order and lived in Sir John's trousers, which he would tuck into his socks to stop Bryan falling out. Visitors to Honington, while regarding this as a fashionable eccentricity, would be struck dumb to see their guide's waistband and shirt on the move, as Bryan clambered upward to kiss his master's ear. During dinner parties Bryan slept in Johnny's smoking-jacket pocket, occasionally making a guest appearance, scuttling down the table between the silver and glass to stretch his legs.

Johnny was devoted to Bryan and quite distraught when the ferret went missing after an orgy of ducks. 'I was heartbroken and did not put it in *The Times* for three days in case he returned, which was very lucky as he had gone to sleep in the dovecote after sucking the blood from three ducks.'

Since Bryan's demise the conducted tours of Honington have not had quite the same éclat, although Sir John, accompanied by the dachshunds, is a charming guide. The house is open on Wednesdays and Bank Holiday Mondays between May and September but, if the Wiggins collect more than £15, they celebrate by buying a lobster in the village for supper. The house is rich in marvellous plasterwork. The hall has an arabesque ceiling, with a sunburst and representations of the elements. On the end walls are two Trojan scenes featuring Aeneas and four panels depicting the Arts, together with some elaborate rococo brackets. The plasterer may have been Charles Stanley, an Anglo-Danish sculptor who left England in 1747.

Most remarkable is the octagonal saloon, constructed about 1751–2, where the design of the amateur (gentleman) architect John Freeman was rather overtaken by that of the executant architect William Jones. The high dome and imposing doors are basically Palladian to which Jones, in extravagant mood, added looking glasses and corner drops of the wildest rococo. Architectural historian John Cornforth has identified the lower drops as representing the elements and seasons, but the significance of the plasterwork in the dome remains a mystery. When the whole house was found to be riddled with dry rot Johnny and Sarah Wiggin, the dogs and the ferrets had to endure two years of restoration work. Section after section of the plaster had to be cut out, rebacked and replaced after treatment of the structure behind. Most of the woodwork had to be dismantled and the floor rebuilt as well. This work revealed the drawing for the original scheme, the first time such an under-drawing had come to light in England.

After restoration of the plasterwork had been completed John Cornforth wrote in *Country Life*: 'How wonderful it is to sit in [the saloon] – or better still lie on the floor – and let one's eye wander from Vulcan to a water spaniel and from Winter's wind to Summer corn and puzzle over why Hercules should have left his lion skins over the doors and his helmet and club in the ceiling. And surely only in an English house would one find Venus being drawn across the ceiling by a Neapolitan painter and a country fox almost within reach of a good fire.'

The dogs could very easily lie on the floor and admire these marvels, but their real interest lies in the churchyard. The church alongside Honington, attributed to Sir Christopher Wren, is in a country setting and the gravestones hold all kinds of delights, although Sir John does his best to discourage the dachshunds from retrieving the flowers on the graves, by giving them the rubber effigy of an eminent politician to play with instead.

Each evening Sonia, known to Sir John as 'my treasured one', leads the family procession upstairs where she lives at the bottom of the Wiggins' bed, wound round their feet like a hot water bottle. The dogs never leave Honington and at the end of one happy day can confidently look forward to more sightseers, more rabbiting with the ferrets and more romps in the graveyard on the morrow.

BELOW: *Overlooked by the severe busts of the twelve emperors of Rome – one of which still conceals a certain piece of underwear left by a weekend guest.*

Minus

THE HON. WILLIAM PETTY-FITZMAURICE

'EVERY night at school, before I go to sleep, I look at the photograph and say, "I wish more than anything in the world that you were here with me."'

The photograph is a portrait of Minus, an elegant black Labrador, taken for thirteen-year-old William Petty-Fitzmaurice by his elder brother Simon.

At home at Bowood, near Calne in Wiltshire, where William's family have lived for more than 220 years, the boy and his dog are inseparable. 'Minus does everything with me. He gets up when I get up. He's dead lazy in the morning and hates to leave my bed. He's really meant to sleep on the floor, of course.' Minus came into William's life six years ago, the result of collusion between William and his nanny and companion Richenda. 'As William is so much younger than his brother and sisters, it was important for him to have someone to cuddle, a real friend.' Richenda's father breeds Labradors and Minus was the runt of a litter.

Pressure was gently brought to bear on William's father, the Earl of Shelburne, a man not particularly partial to dogs. But as William's seventh birthday was approaching, Lord Shelburne agreed on a Labrador as a present provided Richenda was reponsible for the puppy and it was confined to the nursery, well away from the precious sculptures and family heirlooms collected by William's great-great-grandfather, the fifth Marquess of Lansdowne, when he was Viceroy of India.

ABOVE: *Minus has already had three wives; one was his mother and another his sister.*

LEFT: *William at the new front door of Bowood House.*

ABOVE: *'I am training Minus myself.'*

So father and son went to inspect the litter. William remembers: 'I showed Daddy my choice, the runt, and he was horrified and thought I'd made a terrible mistake, but I promised him that Minus would be the best.' Minus rewarded this faith by promptly escaping from his nursery stronghold. 'When he was a tiny puppy Minus disappeared. He could hardly walk but had found his way to Daddy's bedroom and clambered on to the bed where I found him fast asleep.'

When William first went away to school, Minus firmly tucked a large teddy into the bed in lieu of his master and lay protectively on top of it. He was bored during William's term-time absence and did another dis-appearing act. He was found sightseeing in the laboratory where on 1 August 1774 Dr Joseph Priestley discovered oxygen gas.

A keen outdoor dog, Minus appreciates the garden rather more than the house. Few dogs have the run of some fifty acres of rhododendron woods in a park which was once a royal hunting ground and part of the dower lands of the Queen of England. Capability Brown was summoned to Bowood to landscape the park in 1757, three years after the property had been acquired by the second Earl of Shelburne. Now the lawns sweep down to the lake and, in spring, daffodils surround the Doric temple by the water's edge. But William and Minus are happiest in the autumn, in the hunting and shooting season. 'My favourite sport at Bowood is shooting,' says William. 'I'm training Minus myself and he loves duck shooting. We spend hours in the boat on the lake and he talks and grunts and is the best companion. I think Minus is much better than girls.'

William has decided views on love and marriage both for himself and Minus. 'I would never marry anyone who didn't like dogs or who was anti-bloodsports. Minus has already had three wives, one was his mother and another his sister. Dogs don't have feelings like us, no morals saying "you must not", so they don't realise who their mother is. They just think she's rather nice.

'My father has said definitely no more dogs, but one dog I hope to have is a puppy from Minus. I would like a farm with five dogs, twelve chickens, two hundred sheep, fifteen rams, two or three horses and fifty cows. I would get the milk, the wool, the eggs, butter and cheese but I wouldn't be a self-sufficient farmer. We've just been learning about that at school.'

At the word school, Minus always looks miserable. 'When he sees me packing he won't play, he refuses to talk to anyone and tries to get into my suitcase. He sometimes comes with me on the journey to school.' Without his young master Bowood seems bleak for Minus. Nor does he enjoy the unqualified approval of the present-day members of the family. Arabella, William's sister, was alienated when Minus cocked his leg into her chest of drawers. She says she would prefer a snake to a dog.

So Minus spends a lot of time with Richenda at her home, waiting for the telephone to ring. When William comes home for half term the first thing he does is ring up Richenda. 'Minus always knows if it is William on the telephone and frets until he can go back to Bowood.'

BELOW: *'We spend hours in the boat on the lake and he talks and grunts and is the best companion.'*

Jo-Jo, Bizzie and Ba-Ba

LADY SAUNDERS

DOGS, PLEASE KEEP OFF THE GRASS. THANK YOU.

THIS discreet request is centre stage on Katie Boyle's immaculately manicured lawn. The television star, agony aunt and member of Battersea Dogs Home Committee loves all dogs, but has become a great poodle-fancier. 'I never liked poodles – in fact, I never particularly liked people who had poodles, but ever since I've rescued two members of this breed, I have become utterly besotted by them. Poodles are incredibly intelligent, the most adaptable of companions, and the only dogs who enjoy being laughed at.'

Ba-Ba, the black sheep from the Dogs Home, was found wandering last year in Bromley, and faced the world with bared teeth until she joined Katie's pack and regained her confidence. Bizzie-Liz was taken to Katie's vet with a broken leg, the result of a kick from her previous owner. 'Both dogs looked nothing like they do today,' says Katie, and the 'before' and 'after' pictures prove this point. Katie inherited Jo-Jo, a West Highland terrier, from her husband's late wife, which makes him her 'legal and official step-dog'.

This fluffy flotilla follow enquiringly in Katie's wake as a film crew record a day in her life. The morning's mail tumbles out from a sack. Even while reading, Katie is in perpetual motion. The dogs follow her to the bathroom where they obviously feel among friends. Under the plate glass on her dressing table and chest of drawers are photographs of pets, past and present, of all shapes and sizes. 'I decided when I married for the

ABOVE: *The flotilla settled.*

LEFT: *China tea and chocolate cake – rare treats.*

51

ABOVE: *Bizzie at home on a very wet day.*

RIGHT: *Jo-Jo resting. Soon after this picture was taken Jo-Jo died peacefully in Katie's arms.*

third time that it might be more tactful to record my life in dogs – not men.' She points to the photo and to a blob on the top of a Pekinese's head. 'Look, there's a tiny dunnock, a hedge sparrow. I rescued that in Switzerland. It was a fledgling being stalked by a predatory cat. The trouble was that he never had a cage – just a chocolate box lined with tissues and cotton wool, and he always thought he was a dog and hated other birds. I took him to Eaton Square once to try and wean him but, when a sparrow swooped, he dived for the furry undercarriage of my peke.'

Katie looks at a pastel painting of her beloved Yorkshire terrier, Tessa. 'She was put to sleep in my arms some years ago and, of course, every time I have to give a pet this greatest and final proof of my love, I swear I'll never have another because I can't stand the heartbreak. But then I realise this would be very selfish because the dogs I refuse to take home might fall into the wrong hands.'

At tea-time, Katie produces a plastic mat emblazoned Bone Appetite and pours tea – white with one lump – for the dogs, into a bowl of their own. Ba-ba gets in there first and comes up, beard dripping. Bizzie advances and finishes what is left. She steps back with not a drop on her whiskers. 'I swear if Bizzie was a woman she would crook her little finger.' Katie smiles. Tea doesn't appeal to Jo-Jo, but she gulps down a piece of cake, then retires to her basket. Replete with Earl Grey, the black and white minstrels snuggle into Katie's navy suede jacket. They obviously assume that, since she is wearing the matching skirt, she is unlikely to go anywhere without it.

Katie is involved not only in Battersea Dogs Home, the People's Dispensary for Sick Animals (for whom Ba, Bizzie and she made a television appeal for much-needed funds), the Animal Welfare Trust and the National Canine Defence League, but also Pro-Dogs – an association which attempts to instil a sense of responsibility into would-be dog owners. She has rescued many dogs herself – from dustbins, from plastic bags, from motorways – and she has simply appropriated one or two which she felt would be better off in her care. 'I always seem to be rehabilitating and then re-homing various dogs. Peter, my husband, is absolutely wonderful about my orphans; I came home once at dawn with a lurcher who was barely skin and bone, and when our housekeeper brought in our breakfast I heard him ask very gently, "Am I mistaken, or have we got another dog today?"'

Stars of television and radio.

Melba

Mr Peter Cadbury

THE Great Dane sat motionless, as if cast in bronze, her beautiful face creased into a hundred dark, worried furrows. The object of her concern was a tiny stunt aeroplane hurtling down the mown grass runway into the distance, her master at the controls. The plane lifted and disappeared into the blue sky, reappearing minutes later, upside down, for a fly past. The dog remained stock-still, the anxiety in her eyes more than that of any doting wife. The plane landed and the pilot clambered out, beaming with the exhilaration of the stomach-churning flight and pleasure in his dog's boisterous welcome.

Melba is totally faithful to the man in her life. Peter Cadbury believes there is nothing like a Dane and has never been without one. Melba accompanies her master everywhere: land, sea and, when possible, air. Staring at cows from 500 feet fascinates her. She accompanies him on the golf course and can occasionally be seen gracing the deck of a motor cruiser, despite the fact that a swan on the river Hamble once had the temerity to hiss at her. No man, beast or bird had ever been so offensive, but she rose above it womanfully.

'Melba is extremely intelligent, she listens with rapt attention to everything I say, understands me perfectly and, unlike so many beautiful girls, does not argue,' says Peter. She has her own sofa in his study at Armsworth Hill in Hampshire, and her own five-foot double bed built into the boiler room. Any suggestion that she is pampered or spoilt is

ABOVE: *Melba is totally faithful to the man in her life.*

RIGHT: *Peter and Melba in the hall of Armsworth Hill.*

ABOVE: *Crossed paws are typically Great Dane.*

treated by her master with the contempt it deserves.

Great Danes are kings in the canine world. An adult dog will stand at least 30 inches (76 cm) tall and weigh 120 pounds (54.5 kg). They are first recorded around 3000 BC when Egyptian hieroglyphs depict dogs similar to the Great Dane. It is claimed that Phoenician traders spread the mastiffs throughout the Mediterranean, but the Germans believe invading Roman legions brought the forerunner of the Great Dane to their country in the first century. German noblemen used Great Danes for hunting boar during the Middle Ages. Frederick VII of Denmark (1808–63) appointed a counsellor, one Klemp, to reinstate the *Dansk Hund* which had become a rare breed. The German Chancellor Otto von Bismarck chose Great Danes as pets and bodyguards.

Peter Cadbury's first Great Dane was Tory, rescued from a dogs' home

ABOVE: *Was Melba's ancestor a sheepdog?*

because he had a deformed foot. Tory was succeeded by Marcus, then Bertie, all dogs with brindle markings. 'When Bertie died I was devastated and decided I could not go through the torment again. A Great Dane's lifespan in comparatively short and I was heartbroken. Then I was presented with this small, silky bundle, all wrinkles and huge feet and, appropriately, the colour of milk chocolate. She was irresistible and altogether different from her predecessors.' Milk chocolate matured to the colour of melba toast, and so she was christened.

Dame Melba co-habits with Aggro the cat who will sit between Melba's paws in front of the fire, cleaning her teeth with his claws. The dog relishes this curious form of dental flossing; it sends her to sleep, with Aggro as a pillow.

Someone is employed at Armsworth Hill solely to feed and amuse

Melba when Peter Cadbury is away. She occasionally accompanies him to London. Melba's knowledge of the city is strictly limited to Cadogan Square, with an occasional visit to Rotten Row for brisk exercise. There was one unfortunate expedition with Peter to South Audley Street where Melba fell foul of the law. Nature called, and having neglected to read the notices restricting such activity on the pavement, Melba did what she had to do. Observing her, a police constable also felt obliged to do his business and accosted the owner who was rapidly disappearing down South Street. Peter denied all knowledge of the unhappy Melba who, not amused, made it quite clear to the constable that she was closely related to the gentleman helping him with his enquiries. All was forgiven, although Melba thought it quite ridiculous that the policeman recommended a lead which, presumably, had to be attached to that undignified accessory, a collar.

As a result, Melba was treated to the cautionary tale of her predecessor, Marcus, who had committed the same offence in William Street to the great disgust of a shopkeeper who rushed out brandishing a shovel and instructed Peter Cadbury to scoop the poop. He could hardly refuse but he deposited the shovel's hefty contents down a convenient manhole which, less conveniently, had a man in it.

Peter and Melba's relationship is exclusive: 'One Great Dane is a friend and companion; two are a pack and they revert to being dogs, rather than people.' Melba is a Very Important Person. She takes precedence in Peter Cadbury's life over children and wives; he can lavish affection on her unreservedly. 'You only get what you give, that goes for most things in life. No-one who is just a taker can expect to get out of life what it can offer to a man who gives. And that applies to dogs more than people.'

The runway doubles as a perfect driving range and green.

Jess

MRS ROBERT SKEPPER

JESS is a working collie on a seaside farm in Suffolk which she shares with turkeys, geese, horses, sheep, cats, other dogs, two partridges and an orphan owl.

Jess belongs to Hannah Skepper, a modern day Dr Doolittle who breeds bloodstock horses and keeps about 200 Welsh sheep near Woodbridge. Situated in a maze of Suffolk dykes and bordered by the sea wall that runs along the East Anglian coast, the farm is distinguishable for miles by a Martello tower built at the time of the Napoleonic wars. The tower was designed to prevent hostile landings on the coast and is the northernmost in a chain of towers built within sight of one another from Suffolk to Devon.

Jess is a border collie, bred to herd sheep, but also talented at hunting mice and moles. She has a rich brown and white rough coat which is, perhaps, a legacy from her great-grandmother who was a Lassie-type rough collie. Hannah has trained Jess herself and the dog responds to commands by voice and hand signals. She is particularly deft at separating a sheep that needs attention from the flock and enjoys lambing time. She can instantly drop to the ground with the breed's characteristic stealth in order to control her flock. 'Jess saves me hours of running and effort by her speed and quickness, but she is *not* a single-minded sheepdog up to the standard of *One Man and His Dog*,' says Hannah. However, the competitors in the BBC television programme might not be

ABOVE: *Expert moler.*

LEFT: *Jess, Hannah and Percy, a large, fierce turkey.*

RIGHT: *Hannah has trained Jess herself and the dog responds to voice and hand signals.*

LEFT: *Gentle Jess, the perfect working collie.*

so good at herding geese or encouraging horses into horse boxes with a neat directional touch to left or right. Jess is also a willing digger of potatoes. 'You just point at the ground and she digs like mad, throwing the potatoes out between her back legs.'

Hannah is gentle with Jess: 'It is essential not to over-discipline collies. They work because they want to please you and because it is a natural instinct.' If she opens a gate, Jess will automatically herd the sheep into the next field without any need for commands. 'A lot of the work they do is intuitive and the commands are very personal. The dog can tell what you want merely from the intonation of your voice.' Border collies are the most popular breed of sheepdog because of their intelligence and ability to work hard.

Indoors, Jess jostles for space in the kitchen with Ben, a fellow sheep-dog, Sandy, an Alsatian belonging to Hannah's husband Robert, the two quails ('If politely requested they will lay eggs for dinner parties') and the pet owl who usually retreats to a perch on the top of the kitchen curtains. The tropical fish are, of necessity, confined to a tank, and any remaining space is filled with the rosettes won at gymkhanas and competitions, a reminder of the horses outside in the stable yard.

The Skeppers are farmers and racehorse owners and breeders and their children all have ponies. Jess is not so horse-mad. 'If I'm working a young horse she will just go home,' says Hannah. Jess prefers activities she can participate in, like gardening. Collies have acute hearing and she can detect moles tunnelling under the lawn. 'She will run along above a section of tunnels, following them, and then apply her digging skills – which is not always popular.' In the summer she goes to the beach at Aldeburgh. 'It's a sort of retirement town, a preparation for the world beyond, full of retired ambassadors and colonels, but the beach is wonderful,' says Hannah. Jess occasionally goes hunting on the river bank near home. The sails of the boats on the water can be seen at the end of the garden of Ferry Farm.

'Some collies are a menace because they drive things all day long; they have to be driving something and cannot leave well alone. But Jess is content to take a back seat and let Ben do some showy work.' Ben is still young and was first trained by Hannah's mother. There was rather a problem when he arrived at Ferry Farm because the commands given to a dog are so personal. 'He collected the sheep beautifully but I could not get him to let them go. I rang my mother and asked, "How do I get the brake off?" and she said, "You just say 'Ben' or 'Good boy, Ben'." But I had tried both without success. He knew my mother, and exactly what she wanted, and it took several days before he realised what my different ways of saying Ben meant.'

Jess knows exactly what her mistress means by every gesture. 'I never say that I'm going out on the farm, I just get up and she's right there behind me. Yet if I'm going in and out of the house she doesn't bother to follow me.' Jess's companionable nature extends to all her fellow creatures down on the farm. She must be one of the few dogs who can view her mistress embracing a large, fierce turkey (called Percy) with equanimity.

Hannah, the modern day Doctor Doolittle, breeds bloodstock as well as sheep, turkeys and geese.

Smoky, Shadow, Spark, Myth, Fable, Diamond, Kelpie, Geordie and Blackie

HM THE QUEEN AND HM QUEEN ELIZABETH, THE QUEEN MOTHER

THE Welsh corgi and the Royal Famiy joined forces fifty years ago. '1933 was the year of the corgi,' writes the Countess of Longford in *Elizabeth R.* It was also the year that Hitler came to power but, more happily, the year the future George VI (then Duke of York) bought Dookie from the Rozavel kennels in Surrey.

Princess Elizabeth, only seven years old, had fallen in love with a corgi belonging to Viscount Weymouth's family. The breed was a novelty, little known outside South Wales, and Princess Elizabeth enlisted the support of her sister, Princess Margaret, to persuade their parents that they had to have one of the charming, mischievous, foxy little dogs.

The Duke and Duchess of York needed little persuading and Mrs Thelma Gray, breeder of the Weymouths' dog and pioneer of the breed, supplied the first Royal corgi, Rozavel Golden Eagle. He was known as Dookie by Mrs Gray because he acted aristocratically even as a puppy. Three years later Dookie acquired a wife, also from Mrs Gray, called Rozavel Lady Jane. The royal marriage of convenience was unproductive, but Jane made a successful visit to another Rozavel dog and, on Christmas Eve, at Windsor, she produced puppies, two of which, Crackers and Carol, were kept to become King George's and Queen Elizabeth's pets during the war. Mrs Gray lives in Australia and is still breeding corgis.

After having been brought up with corgis, Princess Elizabeth was given

ABOVE: *Great Grandfather Geordie.*

RIGHT: *Four generations.*

LEFT: *The summer house, known as the Eagle's Nest.*

PREVIOUS PAGE: *The Queen going home.*

ABOVE: *Discipline.*

one of her own, Susan, as an eighteenth birthday present in 1944. Susan accompanied Princess Elizabeth and Prince Philip on their honeymoon. The present royal canine dynasty comes from Susan and a litter sired by another of Mrs Gray's champions, Rozavel Lucky Strike. Her Majesty The Queen now has corgis which are the ninth generation of Susan's direct descendents – Smoky, Shadow, Spark, Myth, Fable, Diamond and Kelpie.

The Queen is one of the most experienced breeders of Pembrokeshire corgis. She always chooses the sire herself, aiming for good looking puppies that maintain the red colour of the original Pembrokes. Owners of suitable studs are asked to bring their dogs to Windsor so that the Queen can make her choice. The Queen also has her own unique breed of dorgis, a cross between the Pembrokeshire bitches and Princess Margaret's longhaired dachshund Pipkin. The current dorgi members of the royal household are Piper, who is longhaired, and Chipper, who is smooth-coated and the only male among the Queen's dogs.

74   SMOKY, SHADOW, SPARK, MYTH, FABLE, DIAMOND, KELPIE, GEORDIE AND BLACKIE

Her Majesty Queen Elizabeth The Queen Mother has two corgis, Geordie and Blackie. All the dogs get on well together and travel *en masse* by car, Land Rover, train and aeroplane between their four homes – Windsor Castle, Buckingham Palace, Sandringham and Balmoral. A particular treat in the summer is to go to the Queen Mother's Aberdeenshire home Birkhall, where she has a never-ending supply of chocolate drops for good dogs. Birkhall was built by Captain Charles Gordon in 1715, at the time of Bonnie Prince Charlie. Queen Victoria and the Prince Consort bought the house in 1848, and for some time it was lived in by Sir Digton Probyn, Queen Victoria's comptroller. The Queen Mother moved to Birkhall around 1953. Two years later a large new wing was built by A. Graham Henderson, which added a dining room with additional bedrooms above. In 1983 a new kitchen wing was built by Professor Dunbar Naismith.

Summer days at Birkhall are spent in the garden. Both the Queen and the Queen Mother relax by walking the dogs. The Queen uses Smoky's natural retrieving abilities to pick up birds after shoots in the royal parks.

The Queen feeds the dogs herself whenever her schedule permits, but when she is away or on a royal tour, they go to the wife of a senior Windsor Great Park official who treats them like her own, cares for any sick or in-season corgi, supervises the whelpings and cares for the puppies. Litters are only bred to carry on the strain, and the puppies are never sold, but only given to good permanent homes. There is a royal corgi currently living in New York. Another, Windsor Loyal Subject, went to Mrs Gray in Australia and has won two challenge certificates. Windsor is the prefix under which all the Queen's corgis are registered with the Kennel Club.

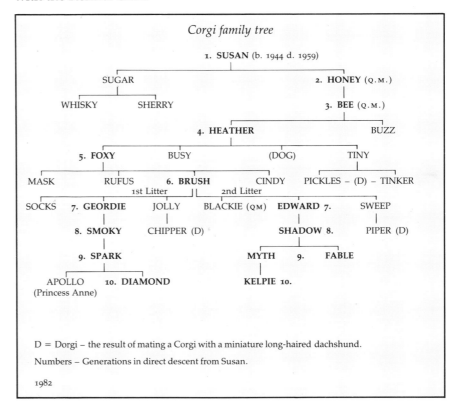

Corgi family tree

1. SUSAN (b. 1944 d. 1959)

SUGAR   2. HONEY (Q.M.)

WHISKY   SHERRY   3. BEE (Q.M.)

4. HEATHER   BUZZ

5. FOXY   BUSY   (DOG)   TINY

MASK   RUFUS   6. BRUSH   CINDY   PICKLES – (D) – TINKER
   1st Litter   2nd Litter

SOCKS   7. GEORDIE   JOLLY   BLACKIE (QM)   EDWARD 7.   SWEEP

8. SMOKY   CHIPPER (D)   SHADOW 8.   PIPER (D)

9. SPARK   MYTH   9.   FABLE

APOLLO   10. DIAMOND   KELPIE 10.
(Princess Anne)

D = Dorgi – the result of mating a Corgi with a miniature long-haired dachshund.

Numbers – Generations in direct descent from Susan.

1982

Chocolate time.

Exercise time at Gatcombe Park.

ABOVE RIGHT: *'Where have you been?'*

Apollo, Random and Laura

HRH The Princess Anne, Mrs Mark Phillips

APOLLO the corgi is a four-year-old refugee from Buckingham Palace, Random a cast-off hound from the Dumfrieshire hunt, and Laura a lurcher who is a coward. They all belong to HRH The Princess Anne, Mrs Mark Phillips, and live at Gatcombe Park her eighteenth-century house in Gloucestershire.

Apollo is usually introduced to visitors bottom first, as he is permanently stuck down rabbit holes. The short back legs and the busy front diggers work in unison investigating the contents of any burrow. His efforts are always frustrated, a fact of country life which Apollo accepts with great good humour. Son of Her Majesty The Queen's corgi Spark, Apollo is a great favourite of Master Peter Phillips. All three dogs are good with children but Apollo is a comic – a reddish, furry ball who challenges you to make any unfavourable comparison with the sun god after whom he is named.

Random also has a distinguished pedigree. The Dumfrieshire breed of hounds is a mixture of French and English foxhounds and some blood-hound. The breed was formed by Sir John Buchanan-Jardine after the First World War, specially for his hunt. The Dumfrieshire kennels are still at his family home, Castle Milk. By 1939 all the hounds were black and tan and had a different temperament to orthodox English foxhounds. 'They're more friendly, more attached to people and have deeper voices. My father always wanted the deeper voice,' says Sir Rupert Buchanan-

Jardine, who now carries the hunt. The French are particularly interested in the Dumfrieshire hound and Sir Rupert has toured France looking at packs of hounds to breed with his own. Random has a lot of French blood; her great-great-great-great grandsire on both sides was Rixensart, a Gascon-Saintongeois bred by Prince de Merode and imported by Sir John. More recently, Random's ancestors have the musical names so typical of English packs – Taffeta and Tatler, Radiant, Radium and Ravish.

Random, now aged seven, received a normal upbringing as a hound but on her first outing to a meet decided such sociability was not for her. She did not care for the noise or the people and stayed firmly in the van,

ABOVE: *Refreshing the parts other dogs can't reach.*

ABOVE: *Privileged positioning.*

refusing to budge. Fortunately Princess Anne, who had previously owned a Dumfriesshire hound, was looking for another and Random, the gentle hound that would not hunt, was an ideal candidate. The Princess was presented with the dog by Sir Rupert Buchanan-Jardine and, although it took the hound a little while to become accustomed to domestic life – 'If you shouted at her she spent a penny and she made nests in the beds,' recalls Princess Anne – Random's surroundings are now far more congenial than any hunt kennel. In between accompanying the Princess on her twice daily rides, Random can nap on one of a pair of tapestry chairs in the flag-stoned hall of Gatcombe, among the rocking

RIGHT: *Laura.*

horse, the doll's pram (complete with doll), Peter and Zara Phillips's soft toys, a grandfather clock and a large lampshade to which an impressive collection of rosettes has been skilfully pinned.

Laura the lurcher naps in the other chair. 'They are the only chairs in the house on which the dogs are allowed,' says Princess Anne. All three dogs sleep outside.

Laura, also aged seven, is graceful and alert and another of the Princess's riding companions. She follows her mistress, perhaps enjoying a bathe in the home-made water jump in preference to the more traditional lurcher pursuits of hunting hares and game. 'She is a born coward,' says the Princess affectionately.

The dogs all lead a fit, healthy outdoor life at Gatcombe, but while Random and Laura are as dedicated to riding as their mistress, Apollo, a typical corgi, chooses to be different. He knows precisely what his little legs are capable of and, as the horse and dogs dash through the park, Apollo will always be found ostentatiously digging to Australia.

Fame

MRS RICHARD BURROWS

ANGELA Burrows sat in her bath and shared the day's successes with her German shepherd dog. Enthroned on a stool by her mistress's side, Fame nuzzled into her own special flannel as Angela performed the nightly ritual of washing first the Alsatian's face, then the equally expectant faces of two spaniels and a sheepdog puppy queuing up behind.

This was the end of a most satisfactory day. Angela's prize mare Easter Silver was in foal to Arab stallion Silver Scenario; the current foals were all successfully weaned; Percy the ram was finally content, having over-ruled a divorce from his wives and, even now, Angela's husband, Richard, would be happily settling himself at White's for a fruitful gossip with his fellow Etonians. The children were away at school and the eighteenth century Suffolk house belonged to Angela and the dogs.

Angela had always wanted a German shepherd dog. 'As a breed they are so intelligent and wonderful and easy, but I didn't dare have one when the children were younger because of all the awful stories. Now I think I made a mistake because Alsatians love to be entertained and the children play with her for absolute hours. The sad thing is that too many people chain Alsatians up so they become bored and then vicious.'

Angela Burrows believes an Alsatian's temperament is all a matter of upbringing. Fame – named after Angela's favourite hit song from the television series – was a highly nervous puppy when she was rescued from her original fate as a show dog. Fortunately Fame's breeder had decided an older puppy was superior to her, and the rejected furry

ABOVE: *Contrary to reputation, Fame is sweet tempered and very lovable.*

LEFT: *Angela and Fame in the drawing room of Barham Hall.*

bundle arrived at Barham Hall trembling with the after-effects of a parvo virus injection. 'It nearly killed her. Being ill in a strange place, it took her ages to get used to everybody. She didn't like me, she didn't like anybody except me, because Alsatians totally attach themselves to one person. Now she would guard me with her life.'

Angela already had two spaniels, Pebble and Pickle, who gave young Fame certain identity problems. 'She thought she was a spaniel and used to get stuck under stools and tables, imagining she was a little dog. The most awful thing was when she got wedged under my dressing table and we had to haul her out with a silk scarf.'

Normally she has beautiful manners and never pushes or barges.' Except when she is trying to be immensely friendly. 'I took her to the park in Ipswich and she hurtled over to a woman with an Afghan who was not best pleased. Fame tried to pick the Afghan up and got in a frightful muddle because the Afghan wanted to play with Fame and her owner didn't want Fame anywhere near her. The more agitated she got, the more hopeless the situation became, and so the woman ended up on the ground with both the Afghan and Fame on top of her.'

Fame is obviously a water dog, blissfully happy on the family's annual bucket-and-spade holiday to Frinton, racing in the waves and seeking sea

BELOW: *Bathtime ritual.*

ABOVE: *Easter Silver, Arab mare in foal to Silver Scenario.*

shells in the breakwaters. She is equally partial to the garden sprinkler, the swimming pool and, of course, Angela's bath. She is also horse-trained. Angela breeds Arabs and every morning Fame, together with Pebble, Pickle and Speedy the sheepdog, escort Angela on her inspection of the stables and monitor her discussion of the day's events with David Skipper, the stud manager. When the horses are foaling 'she sits in the corner, absolutely fascinated, and the horses don't mind.'

Barham Hall is an ideal home for an Alsatian. Built on the site of an old monastery, the rooms are huge and numerous. The house is always full of life. Angela Burrows is full of energy, with Fame her faithful shadow. 'I can walk her anywhere, even in London, and never, never lose her.' Should Angela ever sit down, Fame feigns sleep, ears up like her wolf ancestors. 'They always sleep like that. Flat ears mean she is either very happy and smiley or else in a deep decline. If I tell her off she becomes miserable, because she really wants to please me so much.' The pricked ears are also an early-warning mechanism. 'Fame can hear things none of us can. She always knows when Richard has come home because she can hear the car at the top of the drive.'

Knowing the tricky reputation of the German shepherd breed, it is a delight to see this gentle dog so content after her nervous, sickly puppy-hood. 'She's so obedient. I never have to put her on the leash and she retrieves anything. She particularly loves pheasants. My father-in-law always did swear they were the best gun dogs, but actually you can teach Alsatians to do anything.'

Still, the breed's reputation is formidable and docile Fame can be misunderstood. Huge, burly workmen mending the roof at Barham refused to descend their ladder until she was shut in the house. They may still be up there.

Jacko

LORD OAKSEY

JACKO is a matinée idol. He became a television star in just one afternoon by muscling in on his owner's racing commentary.

Lord Oaksey's car had broken down and, having nowhere to leave the dog, Britain's best-known racing peer was forced to make his TV appearance with the black and tan terrier tucked under his arm. Jacko enjoyed it very much, as did thousands of television racegoers, and he received a gratifying amount of fan mail. Real recognition came in a motorway service station on the Pennines. Having decided that his dog had had its day, John Oaksey asked a friend to accompany him and Jacko in case of further accidents en route to the racecourse. While Lord Oaksey went to make a telephone call, Jacko queued with his minder for an ice cream. A huge lorry driver scrutinised the terrier and said, 'That's Jacko, isn't it?' That was real fame.

With fame came the attendant hazards. It was possibly because of his new status in life that Jacko fell out with a very old and dear companion. Webster, a happy, good-natured Labrador and near neighbour in the little Cotswold village of Oaksey, would often invite Jacko to stay. But one evening there was a disagreement of mysterious origin which prompted a heavyweight fight. Jacko now regards the unfortunate Webster as Enemy Number One. Just a glimpse of him in the distance will reduce the terrier to quivering rage. But then Jacko does specialise in insulting other male

ABOVE: *The matinée idol.*

RIGHT: *Jacko feels he has a superior claim to the ball since, unlike most tennis players, he can execute four somersaults with it clenched firmly between his teeth.*

dogs at horse shows and team events. He growls ferociously, regardless of the size of his opponent.

John Oaksey is devoted to the Terrier Terror. They travel everywhere together so that Jacko has an encyclopaedic knowledge of Britain's racecourses. He is on first name terms with the authorities and, should Lord Oaksey dare to leave him at home, 'the first question is "How's Jacko?"' Now that his opportunities for stardom have been nipped in the bud, Jacko usually retires to the car after he has inspected the course. Curled up, awaiting his master's return, Jacko can dream of rabbiting. His favourite pastime has been severely curtailed by the advent of middle-age spread. Now it is a frustrated black and tan terrior who, like one of Cinderella's ugly sisters, is frequently found trying to squeeze himself into accommodation designed for a more streamlined individual.

Consolation is a tennis ball. 'The most frustrating time of his life is when we're playing tennis,' says John Oaksey, for Jacko has a keen eye for the ball. Like a Wimbledon spectator, his head swivels from left to right following the match. He feels he has a superior claim to the ball, since, unlike most tennis players, he can execute four somersaults with it clenched firmly between his teeth.

His winter sport is ratting around the jumps of the cross-country course and the maze of golden Cotswold walls that surround Hill Farm. The English black and tan terriers, now extinct, were famed for centuries as rat fighters in the north of England. Jacko is an Irish cousin, bred in Limerick, where they have developed a strain of black and tan hunt terriers that have, in a pleasant Irish way, nothing to do with the hunt. Some are rough-coated, others smooth, and Lord Oaksey owned two bitches before the arrival of Jacko some six years ago. Concerned about Jacko's wellbeing at every level, John Oaksey would like to import a suitable Irish wife for the lad but, to date, Jacko's interest in the opposite sex has been limited to the cows in Hill Farm's patchwork fields, and John has now come to the sad conclusion that the fierce, macho terrier is 'marginally queer'.

The Oaksey family has specialised in gutsy little dogs with a constructive interest in agriculture. 'My father used to drive over to see his cows with my sister's Pekinese, Hickypoo, on a lead. When both of them had satisfactorily inspected the livestock on one such occasion, my father got back into the car with the lead inside but the dog on the end of it, shut outside. It was only after he had driven about a quarter of a mile that he realised what had happened. With great presence of mind Hickypoo had hung on to the lead, lost all his teeth, but survived.'

Jacko may be all brawn on the outside – with the added masculine charm of permanent fleas – but his palate is delicately discriminating. Lord Oaksey claims, 'Jacko is probably the only dog in England to live on a diet of chicken and digestive biscuits every day of his life.'

RIGHT: *Devoted friends.*

Muffin, Mishka, Mufti, Molly, Mitzi, Millie, Mumbo, Bessie and Lara

LAVINIA, DUCHESS OF NORFOLK

LAVINIA, Duchess of Norfolk, has her own family breed of dogs, a cocktail of Pekinese, cairn terrier, cavalier King Charles spaniel and Tibetan spaniel.

It all began with Sherry who was a cross between a peke and a cairn. She married a cavalier King Charles and produced Minnie whose first association with another male peke resulted in Muffin, now nine years old, who belongs to Lavinia Norfolk's daughter Sarah Fitzalan-Howard. Minnie then had an affair with a cairn who begot a heavily moustached daughter, Mishka, now seven, who belongs to Sarah's sister Mary.

Sarah married Muffin to a highly desirable Tibetan spaniel, a pug-nosed dog originally bred by Tibetan Buddhists to turn their prayer wheels and guard their monasteries. Muffin and her exotic swain had Mufti, the only boy in the litter, who was given to Lavinia Norfolk's Nanny while Sarah kept one of his sisters Molly.

Mary Fitzalan-Howard sent the bewhiskered Mishka off to another eligible peke and amongst their five offspring were Mitzi, Millie and Mumbo. Mary kept Mumbo and gave the other two to her mother. Mitzi

LEFT: *The Norfolk family, Muffin, Mishka, Mufti, Mollie, Mumbo, Mitzi and Millie, Bessie and Lara.*

ABOVE: *The bewhiskered Mishka.*

looks like a Shi Tzu, while Millie is tiny and fragile and was overwhelmed with morning sickness after conjugal relations with a Yorkshire terrier.

Overseeing this unique brood are Bessie, Lavinia Norfolk's original Labrador, and Lara, a graceful retriever who belonged to a friend of Sarah's. Bessie came from the Labrador Rescue Society along with two other Labradors, one blind and the other with severe hip displacement, the result of being permanently chained in a kennel. There were severe sores on her legs where she had sat for too long, but the Duchess cured the dog with exercise in Arundel Park.

Lavinia Norfolk is a dog's best friend; she has organised a dog sanctuary at Climping in Sussex, is president of both the Chichester and the Brighton branches of the RSPCA and national president of the National Canine Defence League. All her own dogs are charity workers. They have pioneered the Friends of Climping Sanctuary, a scheme through which happy dogs can help their unlucky counterparts. 'The "friend" dog pays an annual subscription and receives a signed certificate and a medal for his collar,' explains the Duchess. 'Invitations are sent to the friends every year for a party at Arundel cricket ground, dress collar and lead, and they

BELOW: *Lavinia, Duchess of Norfolk with Mitzi on the terrace of Arundel Park.*

are allowed to bring their two-legged parents.' The Climping Dog Sanctuary can only accommodate twelve dogs but it keeps the difficult Alsatian/Labrador crosses as long as possible and takes a dog back if it is unhappy in a new home. Only the saddest, hopeless cases are put down.

Millie's and Mitzi's charity work includes helping disabled children. Lavinia Norfolk believes that dogs can have a therapeutic effect on anyone handicapped or ill. 'The spastics and the young mentally handicapped respond to the dogs. They can bring out more than any human being. I also take them into the hospices. When a friend of mine was ill, she smiled for the first time when I put Mitzi and Millie on her bed. Now they let all the patients have their dogs in for visits. There is one hospice I am president of in Brighton where they gave a dying patient a chihuahua and it literally gave her life. She had to get up to take it into the garden.'

The Duchess and her dogs live in a modern house designed by architect Claude Phillimore and built in Arundel Park twenty-five years ago. Arundel Castle, the vast family seat of the Norfolk family, head of the English peerage for 500 years, is one of the grandest achievements of the Romantic imagination of the eighteenth and nineteenth centuries but

BELOW: *The family line-up.*

LEFT: *Muffin in the herbaceous border, waiting for the rabbit.*

hardly conducive to cosy family living. The Duchess, together with the late Duke, chose the site for their own home near the gallops used by the racehorses in training at John Dunlop's stable below. Trees have now matured to shield the house from the town.

Lavinia Norfolk wanted a long, low house with a main block and two self-contained wings, one for her daughters and the other one for the cook and valet. Now the wings are either closed down or lent to grandchildren or friends. In the garden, clouds of red roses bloom all summer, and there is a large herbaceous border which the dogs believe has been planted specifically for rabbiting purposes. Mumbo and Mishka are in the front line of the hunting pack and can frequently be seen, bottoms up, in a clump of Michaelmas daisies.

As the dogs attend most of the Duchess's charity functions, long walks are essential to counteract the excesses of wine and cheese parties. Once round the park, below the battlements of Arundel Castle, is enough to cure most hangovers. Arundel is only exceeded in solidity and scale by Windsor and Alnwick castles. It first came into the possession of the Fitzalans in 1243 and passed to the Howards on the marriage of Lady Mary Fitzalan, daughter of the twelfth Earl of Arundel, to Thomas, fourth Duke of Norfolk, in 1556. He was later beheaded for attempting to marry Mary, Queen of Scots, and her rosary is among the castle's historic relics. Much of the original castle was destroyed in 1643 during the English Civil War by besieging Parliamentarians, and reconstruction began in the eighteenth century. The result is feudal, grandiose. It is open to the public. Mufti, Molly, Muffin, Mishka, Mitzi, Millie, Mumbo, Bessie and Lara often visit the monumental staterooms – the library is vaulted entirely in mahogany – but they are unimpressed. No number of Van Dyck family portraits could beat rabbiting in the flower bed.

BELOW: *Lara and Mollie, first cousin of Mumbo, Millie and Mitzi.*

Blackie, Tina, Tramp, Slim Jim and Layla

THE BATTERSEA DOGS HOME

IT is a temporary refuge for most of the thousands of dogs taken there each year, but for Blackie, Tina, Tramp, Slim Jim and Layla the Dogs Home, Battersea, *is* home.

Blackie, a mongrel who came in as a stray, was once adopted by new owners but he escaped and returned to Battersea. Now he only goes away on an occasional seaside holiday paid for by admirers. Photographs of Blackie frolicking in the waves have appeared in the *Daily Mirror*, but celebrity did not alter his permanent attachment to the Home and kennel girl June Haynes.

Tina arrived pregnant and had to have a Caesarean section to deliver her thirteen puppies. By the time she recovered, Tina had decided to stay. She has her own bed in the changing room and is never shut in and never alone. The kennel maids keep her company during the day and a watchman is on duty all night. 'She gets more attention that your own dog at home,' says Dot Dockett, Battersea's deputy superintendent. Her puppies found good homes and Tina satisfies her maternal instincts by jumping into boxes. 'All the puppies arrive in boxes, so every time she sees one she thinks it's got puppies in it.'

Layla is a collie cross brought into Battersea with a severe mouth injury

ABOVE: *Born at Battersea.*

LEFT: *From 18 pounds to 80 pounds in a few weeks. Sir Giles Gilbert Scott's Battersea Power Station in the background.*

ABOVE: *Slim Jim exercising a friend.*

and a damaged saliva gland, wounds which took so long to heal that she too became one of this family of orphans.

When Tramp the German shepherd arrived, he only weighed 18 pounds when he should have weighed 80. 'He was all skin and bones, so thin we had to put him on a special bed so that his bones did not touch the floor. His head had sunk in, but the superintendent took him on because he was so pathetic.' Tramp is now fit and well, a fine figure of a dog, back to his normal weight.

William Wadman-Taylor, manager of the Dogs Home, saved Slim Jim's life. He found the German shepherd puppy cowering and unable to walk. 'He was about three or four months old, big enough to walk, but he was absolutely petrified. He was afraid of everything and desperately thin. I had to carry him here. After a while he began to improve and got quite cocky and confident. Then he got an infection. As he was so under-nourished, we didn't give him much of a chance and thought he would probably have to be put down.' Mr Wadman-Taylor decided to reprieve Slim Jim for one week, at the end of which he had recovered. Today Slim Jim is so full of energy and mischief it is hard to believe lack of confidence has ever been one of his problems.

It costs £2000 a day to run Battersea Dogs Home. The 457 kennels usually have more than one dog in them. Long-term inmates have touching appeals pinned to their kennel bars: 'I am very nice and I would like to belong to a family and play in green fields.' Happily only about 15 to 17 per cent of the strays brought in to Battersea remain. 'Most people who come here seeking their own dog find it. The joy of the dog and the owner who never thought they would see each other again is well worth having,' says Mr Wadman-Taylor, who is a retired vet and member of the general committee of the Kennel Club. 'The Kennel Club is at the opposite end of the spectrum to Battersea Dogs Home. It deals with all the pedigree dogs and Battersea deals with all the mutts.'

The Dogs Home has five vans which trundle round London every day except Sunday collecting strays, mainly from police stations. About fifty dogs are brought in each day, and between thirty and forty of the unclaimed or unwanted dogs sold. The minimum fee is £20 and buyers are obliged to have proper identification and fill out a questionnaire. 'If we are not sure where the dogs are going, or what the people are like, we suggest a home visit before they purchase the dog,' says Dot. 'We have a home visitor who goes round and, if we're satisfied, we'll then let the dog go.'

Dogs arriving on the van are inoculated, checked over by a nurse, given a health card and number and then taken off to their blocks where they remain for seven days. If unclaimed by the eighth day, they go for sale. 'As long as the dogs are healthy, they stay here and will be re-homed, not put down,' says Dot. But some dogs, like people, are more attractive than others; whereas the pedigrees and the swashbuckling sort of mongrels

RIGHT: *How can one resist such an appeal?*

will go quickly, the ugly and the old can serve a long sentence behind those bars.

Perhaps saddest of all are the dogs brought in by people insisting they have been found in the street. 'It's not always true. You can tell by the way the dogs pull back to them, but people don't like to admit they're abandoning their own dog,' says Dot. A lot of the new arrivals are very nervous. 'You can't blame them,' says Mr Wadman-Taylor. 'First they're roaming the street, then hiked to a police station, put in a van by a strange person, driven all over London and then taken out of the van to have a needle stuck into them.'

Every dog is a potential carrier of disease, but Mr Wadman-Taylor is thankful that the Dogs Home has never, so far, become so grossly overcrowded that healthy dogs have had to be culled to prevent the spread of illness. A lot of the dogs are injured when they arrive (although cruelty cases are dealt with by the RSPCA), and they are nursed back to health on chicken, fish and rice. Battersea spends £40,000 on dogmeal alone every year.

Specialist pedigree breeds, like Afghans, Great Danes and St Bernards, are referred to the breed club's rescue society. 'They're very, very good because they know all the breeders in the different areas and when the dogs were sold. If the stray dog is a puppy, they'll find out who sold it recently and trace the original owner through the breeder. If all that fails, at least the dog can be adopted by someone who understands the breed,' says Mr Wadman-Taylor.

Christmas and July are the busiest times of year at Battersea Dogs Home. 'July is holiday time and people don't make plans, or can't afford to board their dogs, so they leave them on the side of the road. It is not as callous as you might think, because that minority of the British people know that the majority will rescue their dog and either give it a good home or bring it to Battersea.'

The noise and the smell are appalling, the concrete surroundings drab and bare, but this does not alter the fact that Battersea is a good deed shining in the dog world. Blackie, Tina, Tramp, Slim Jim and Layla give it the ultimate vote of confidence. If they had not liked it, they need not have stayed.

The whole family.

Henry and Basil

MR AND MRS JOHN MENZIES

PAT Menzies was shopping in Harrods when, on a whim, she decided to visit the pet department. She was still in mourning after the death of her fourteenth Pekinese. Her sister had suggested she should now have a sensible dog, like a basset hound, and had even offered to basset-sit in the Menzies' absence so that the new arrival would not have to go to kennels.

Encouraged by this, Pat Menzies braved the cages in Harrods' pet department and asked for a basset hound. 'Amazingly, although they hadn't had any for at least fourteen months, two brother bassets had arrived from Norfolk that morning. I was taken to a tiny cage where there were these two adorable puppies. I looked at them and cuddled them both, but there was one who gave me a very special look that seemed to say "I'm the one for you". I went home unable to make up my mind and related the story to my bewildered husband. He listened patiently and agreed, on sufferance, to come with me to Harrods at 9 am the next day.'

At 9.05 the following morning John Menzies stood in the pet department, considerably annoyed that the puppies had not yet been woken. Eventually two sleepy babies were placed in the Menzies' arms and they put them on the floor to choose the lucky candidate. Henry, having already decided he belonged to Pat Menzies, waddled over to his new mistress. Basil just sat, looking beguiling. Johnny Menzies was touched. He picked up the puppy who wriggled and fell out of his arms, landing on his head on the floor.

LEFT: *Pat, Henry and Basil in the library at Kames.*   105

ABOVE: *Basil looking for security in a flowerbed.*

Pat Menzies remembers: 'We were appalled that he might have hurt himself. Johnny looked at me and I looked at Johnny and the decision was made. We took both puppies, as we couldn't bear the thought of leaving Basil behind.' So John Menzies, who had not wanted a dog at all, ended up with two.

The journey home from Harrods to Scotland was packed with incident. Mrs Menzies, her two small daughters Katie and Cynthia, their two hamsters Apricot and Alice, Henry and Basil and Nanny appropriated a first class railway compartment. 'We hadn't been on the train very long before both dogs were out of their cages, as were both hamsters. The smell was indescribable all the way to Berwick-on-Tweed. I said to Nanny, "I don't think we'll have much difficulty keeping this compartment to ourselves."'

Thus the bassets arrived at their home, Kames, said to be one of the three oldest houses in southern Scotland. Henry and Basil have their own little house in the garden, white like the big house and with roses round the door which sports a brass fox's mask and brush knocker. Inside there are two baskets under a large heat lamp and the walls are of double thickness to ensure warmth. The dogs even have their own back garden, planted with tree lupins and clematis entwined round cottage fencing, with a ramp down from the 'basset flap' to make life easier for these now elderly gentlemen. At the age of fourteen, Basil has a touch of arthritis for which he takes Disprin. The basset flap was an inspired idea to prevent draughts, although at first Pat Menzies had to crawl through it backwards and forwards to give Basil the confidence to use it.

LEFT: *The dog house, complete with basset flap, roses round the door and tree lupins in the garden.*

'We have a perpetual problem with Basil's confidence,' she says. 'Johnny and I agreed about how to bring up the children, but not the dogs. I suppose it was because I've had a dog since I was five and, before Basil, Johnny had only had gun dogs which lived in kennels. So my dogs always slept in the bedroom with me and were hugged and kissed and spoken to as if they were people. Johnny calls it "making an utter fool of myself", because I don't actually notice much difference between my children and my dogs. It's the way I've always felt about them. Henry often clambers up on my knee for a cuddle. But Basil knows he's Johnny's dog and adores him, yet his upbringing has been different. He sits at Johnny's feet and if Johnny puts out a hand and pats him, Basil looks ecstatic, but that's the extent of the demonstrative affection that he gets. I suppose he feels a little sad about this because he's got grumpy as he's got older. I try to help out but it's a little late. I send Henry out into the garden so I can have a love-in with Basil. We cuddle and kiss for about fifteen minutes while watching the tennis on television and he does begin to relax, although he is still unsure of himself and others.'

Basset hounds naturally specialise in looking lugubrious. They are the original Hush Puppies but, long before becoming a modern trademark, bassets were hunting dogs. They may be descended from the ancient French *basset d'Artois*, or have been brought to Europe from Constantinople during the Crusades, but the name may also derive from the first two such dogs in England, who were brought by Lord Galway in 1866 from the Comte de Tournon and whose names were Bassat and 'Balle. Sir Everett Millais, a later breeder, added the bloodhound strain to his basset

BELOW: *Pat Menzies with the boys in front of Kames.*

stock to create the distinctively British breed that look like melancholy judges.

Henry and Basil have certainly lived up to their hunting heritage. Forty-mile jaunts trailing roe deer across the Scottish Borders were not unknown in their youth. Their philandering frequently resulted in nights in police stations or irate farmers' sheds. Even cattle grids proved useless as a way of keeping the dogs at home, since bassets' paws are so large and squashy that the dogs can lumber across the bars. Finally, after years of worry, Pat Menzies received her most welcome birthday present from her husband: a five-foot fence, topped with electric wire and sunk six inches below ground to make Kames Henry-and-Basil-proof. Seven gates with bolts and padlocks allow access to human visitors.

Just to reassure the boys that their hunting days are not quite over, two rabbits live inside the wire and are pursued at regular intervals with much baying. Yet it would seem that the arrangement is quite amicable, since one rabbit always leads, followed by Henry, then Basil, while the other rabbit brings up the rear.

Johnny demonstrating his affection.

Phoebe

MRS DAVID KEITH

TWELVE years ago, when David and Caroline Keith were celebrating their silver wedding with family and friends at the Berkeley Hotel in London, Phoebe arrived in a host of golden daffodils. The black and tan baby long-haired dachshund was screaming with indignation, having been wrested from the warmth of the ladies' loo and deposited in the yellow basket among wet green stalks.

'The basket was presented to David and me like a cake at the end of a birthday party, and I must admit that at the time I thought, Oh God, not a puppy!' remembers Caroline. The thought was fleeting, as Phoebe immediately became an intrinsic part of life at West Barsham, the Keiths' Norfolk home which boasts some of the finest partridge shooting in England.

But Phoebe, a gentle soul, held back from sporting activity and devoted herself to Caroline. One of her ancestors had belonged to Queen Victoria, who refers to her dog Dash in a diary entry in 1833. Phoebe was decidedly a lady-in-waiting sort of dachshund, happiest on her mistress's bed, snuggled among the lace pillows, rather than hunting small animals to earth, something at which dachshunds excel. The daffodils must have made a lasting impression on her as she takes a keen interest in horticulture, padding quietly beside Caroline as she tends the myriad species of house plants and flowers throughout West Barsham Hall.

Phoebe was an only dog, and Caroline and David felt she needed

LEFT: *Caroline and Phoebe on the terrace at West Barham Hall.*

ABOVE: *Dear Phoebe.*

111

companionship of her own sort. But David ruled out the possibility of motherhood. 'He was so besotted by her that there was absolutely no question of her ever having puppies, because he felt there was always a great danger in childbirth. He wasn't worried about me having children, but Phoebe was quite different,' says Caroline. So Phoebe's half-sister, Sophie, was acquired. 'Sophie was the stooge dog and Phoebe the boss, the queen. But it did mean that, if I went away, Phoebe had a friend.'

Then seven years ago disaster struck the little dog. Caroline noticed that one of Phoebe's eyes had become strangely coloured. An eye specialist at the Animal Health Trust in Newmarket diagnosed a malignant tumour and the eye had to be removed. Caroline stayed at the Animal Health Trust, a sophisticated veterinary hospital any person would be proud to be treated in, and held Phoebe's paw while she had her pre-med injection. Nine days after the operation Caroline gently removed the stitches herself. 'I didn't want her to go through the trauma of doctors again, so I clipped them out as she lay in the sun on the lawn.'

Phoebe triumphed over her disability with characteristic patience. Then last year she contracted diabetes. She started drinking frantically and, after sleepless nights battling with the burglar alarm to let Phoebe

BELOW: *Dawdling in the dahlias.*

out into the garden, Caroline took her to the best diabetic animal specialist at the Royal Veterinary College. As a result Phoebe was spayed, put on a rigid diet and condemned to daily insulin injections from the vet. 'I suppose it was desperately wet of me but I just could not do it myself,' says Caroline.

But every day she meticulously measured Phoebe's food, the very best, leanest beef and natural health meal, and weighed the dog on baby scales. In the early morning Caroline could be seen flitting round the lawn in her dressing gown, attempting to collect a specimen from Phoebe in a saucer. She would then carry out daily tests for protein and glucose levels. No human diabetic could have had more loving care and attention.

But on 20 October 1985 Phoebe lost her battle with the disease. Her mistress wrote: 'My darling, beloved, adored little dog died on Sunday morning. I have cried solidly for three days non-stop. She was so well and we thought we'd got this diabetes beaten with the diet and that we were winning. I suppose her heart just gave out. We must be thankful for the glorious years of the most divine animal. We shouldn't have dogs, should we? The agonies of losing them are too much.' Phoebe, wrapped in Caroline's dressing gown, was buried under her favourite tree.

BELOW: *Social secretary.*

Mr Whistle, Lady, Puzzle and family

Mr Loudon Constantine

THE early morning mist lingered round the elegant early eighteenth century rectory on the hill. The village still slept below. But Mr Whistle was wide awake. He was considering what damage he might inflict on a William and Mary tallboy. Mr Brown, Miss Brown, Miss Diamond, Catapult, Flash, Boy, H. and Whitey were rolling in the flower bed; Puzzle had a ball in her mouth and Lady lay with her four paws in the air.

All belong to Loudon Constantine, master of the elegant Buckinghamshire rectory – ten English springer spaniels and one Sheltie sheepdog with a crooked tail which got trapped in a car door when he was a puppy. Loudon is a fisherman, keen shot, antique collector, former owl-tamer at Eton, and the sort of chap who chucked competing in the America's Cup when he heard his spaniel had had puppies.

That was eight years ago when Lady, his prize gun dog, gave birth. The squirming, wriggling mass of Mr Brown, Miss Brown, Miss Diamond, Catapult, Flash, H., Boy and Whitey belong to Puzzle, who spurned her custom-built whelping box to have her puppies under the Adam sideboard in the dining room. From this vantage point Puzzle can enjoy an uninterrupted view of Loudon's collection of dark blue and red Royal Worcester china. It is the Queen Charlotte pattern which spans four

LEFT: *Loudon Constantine and his four-footed family in front of the rectory.*

ABOVE: *An armful of heaven.*

LEFT: *Puzzle is a small, very feminine spaniel with total confidence in her master.*

Worcester periods from the end of the eighteenth century to the beginning of the Victorian era.

It was the first litter that had an electrifying effect on Mr Whistle. Previously believed to be rather effeminate – he always walks on the tips of his toes like a ballet dancer – Mr Whistle became increasingly virile under the happy illusion that he was the father of the puppies. He was later caught *in flagrante delicto* with Lady in the stables, catastrophic news that caused Loudon to cancel all his meetings, close the office and return home frantic. 'It was unthinkable that my wonderful spaniel should have been assaulted by a common collie.' Luckily the union bore no fruit. Mr Whistle was obviously not as virile as he had thought. He went into a deep decline, venting his frustrations on furniture, but only furniture made before 1700. He is very discriminating about the walnut period, and particularly partial to the William and Mary tallboy. Since being subjected to his attentions, it stands, unhappily, on three and a half legs in the hall. 'He hasn't got into the mahogany yet,' says Loudon gloomily.

Lady was the first spaniel to take over his life after a succession of Shi Tzus. She had already won several shooting trials, so Loudon went into vigorous training himself and together they made guest appearances at shoots throughout the country. Once Lady tried to retrieve a salmon in a rather deep river, much to the annoyance of the ghillie who was already up to his armpits in water and in serious risk of drowning. Loudon retorted that 'if my dog wants to retrieve my fish, that is my business.'

RIGHT: *A vantage point – to watch the brood.*

Lady is contrary. Taken to a shooting seminar in Devon with spaniels from all walks of life, she went on strike, lay on her back with her legs in the air and whined piteously until the final test, when she swept the board to demonstrate her supreme contempt for the entire proceedings.

Puzzle is one of Lady's progeny. She conducts her life on the placebo principle; whether feeding her puppies or sitting on her Queen Anne walnut chair in the drawing room, Puzzle always has a ball in her mouth. It's doubtful if this makes her a riveting conversationalist, but she can be relied upon to make up the numbers at dinner. To see an empty chair is to sit on it.

Puzzle is a small, very feminine spaniel, with total confidence in her master. He supervised her whelping, maternity manual in hand, reviving one weak pup in the Aga, sadly failing with another, despite mouth-to-mouth resuscitation. Together they have taken the puppies for their first outing: an educational drive in the car. 'I pointed out all the landmarks and they had a wonderful time destroying the back seat,' says Loudon. Puzzle's favourite spot for baby-minding is just below the mellow, yellow brick garden wall, spread with tumbling pink roses like a child's frilly party dress. Mr Brown and Catapult swing on the low branches of a young blue cedar; Miss Diamond whimpers, after her first acquaintance with nettles; Boy gets covered in burrs and the others play tug of war with an old turquoise scarf. If their behaviour becomes too boisterous Puzzle confiscates their toys, removing the scarf and one old slipper to her basket.

Mr Whistle is taking a stepfatherly interest, having discovered his limitations. Indeed Shelties are thought to have been used as baby-sitters in the past. They may have originated from Yakkis, Icelandic dogs brought by whalers to the Shetland Islands where, for centuries, they herded livestock and were renowned for devotion to their master, family and home.

Lady and Puzzle tolerate Mr Whistle benignly, unlike Leo, Loudon's fourth and last Shi Tzu. 'Leo and Mr Whistle hated each other,' says Loudon. 'When Leo was thirteen and very old, he said to himself one morning, "I'm going to die today, I'm rheumaticky and today's the day." Then, out of the corner of one eye, he saw Mr Whistle and became so obsessed with the idea of taking one more bite out of the dreadful imposter that he got a new lease of life. He would crawl up behind Mr W. to give a really good nip and this went on for three years until, one day, he woke up and said, "I think I really am going to die today," and saw Mr Whistle and again changed his mind, but his last tooth fell out and that really was the day. Hatred prolongs life in the dog world.'

Now it is Mr Whistle's turn to enjoy a peaceful old age. His youth has been served, he has had his day and it has been a fine one.

Adoration of the master.

119

The Boiled Owl

Mrs Alexander McEwen

Dear Felicity,

The Owl is a bearded collie, and was christened 'Guffo Bollito' or Boiled Owl (trans. Ital.). Otherwise known as Owlie, Owler, Guffo, Guffolino etc. She lives in our large Victorian pile, where she moved with her owners two years ago. She infinitely prefers large house living and the immediate contact with rabbits and hares. The occasional encounter with a sheep is a very favourite pastime – and a hazard for her owners.

She has assembled a court of one Dandie Dinmont and, latterly, her granddaughter, a toffee-coloured beardie called Minnie (ex. Memphis Minnie). She loathes general or private conversation when she is not included, so prevents this by barking continuously until the participants are forced to capitulate. She is reaching the autumn of her life and is faintly arthritic.

She and I have agreed it would be a fitting tribute to her star-studded life to feature in your book. She is too tired to write herself, as she had to interrupt the conversation of eighteen people all weekend.

With love from Cecilia

Bones – real, rubber and biscuit – littered the hall of the Victorian mansion in Ayrshire and the Boiled Owl was, true to the letter, barking continuously. Frenzied activity in the kitchen had given away the fact that

ABOVE: *Settled among the gunnera leaves on the bank of the River Stinnchar.*

LEFT: *Cecilia, the Boiled Owl, Memphis Minnie and Dimmie in the newly-decorated drawing room at Bardrochat.*

121

twenty-five Americans were coming to lunch en route to 'do' Scottish castles, and she disapproved vociferously. Nor was the Boiled Owl happy that she had inadvertently been bathed in cod liver oil. 'With a name like Mirrorcoat of course I thought it was shampoo, not some stuff to put in her food. Complete disaster. I couldn't understand why it didn't foam up.' Cecilia McEwen is brisk, breezy and unabashed by Owlie's deep decline when confronted by the hairdryer.

Bardrochat is a red sandstone Scots mansion perched above the village of Colmonell. It was designed by Robert Lorimer and built in 1865 by Robert McEwen, grandfather of Cecilia's husband Alexander. During Alexander's childhood Bardrochat was the family's seaside house; in winter they retreated to Marchmont, an Adam house at Greenlaw, East Lothian.

Cecilia braces herself to banish the Boiled Owl to the car before the arrival of the Americans whom she entertains at Bardrochat House on their tours of Scotland organised by the American Museum in Bath. 'The trouble is that Owlie just bloody well interferes if you are talking. At lunch she'll simply sit and bark, bark, bark. It's so difficult when you are trying to describe the intimate details of some Scottish castle to a nice American woman who has never been here before.' The Boiled Owl ingratiates herself into Cecilia's lap. 'Oh dear, she thinks she is a puppy or a lap dog. Do look, you *must* see every feature of her wonderful face. Sitting here is quite her favourite position but she'll suffer terribly from the heat *any* minute. It must be her fur, or maybe she's menopausal – she's now aged twelve.'

Guffo Bollito came into Cecilia's life because she was supposedly like the doggie in the window with the waggerly tail. 'I saw one in an antique shop near us in London, always prancing around in the window, always absolutely enchanting, nothing like the Owl I fear. Finally I went in and said, "What is that dog? I've been looking at it for months and months," and they said it was a bearded collie. So I hunted down breeders and eventually found the Owl near Basingstoke, and she's never looked back since she came to Scotland.' Neither have the McEwens. 'All the McEwens are famous for loathing dogs, they never had dogs in the house until Owlie. But Alexander adores her, although possibly not quite so much when he returns puffing and sweating off the hill after she has rounded up the odd sheep. I'm afraid that, confronted with a sheep, the Owl is unstoppable.'

Until the First World War bearded collies, originally known as hairy mountain dogs, were used as working sheepdogs in the Borders, but they were superseded by the smooth collie because the snow and ice matted so badly in the fur on their chrysanthemum-style feet. But the working beardie is making a come-back, which does not, as far as Cecilia McEwen is concerned, include the Boiled Owl. She has been trained by a shepherd, with the beneficial result that she will not now leave Bardrochat on a private sheep hunt. 'But if you're walking through sheep, you have to wave your stick and shout until you're blue in the face. She's so fast, like all collies, and gets so excited, and the sheep are so stupid, it's not surprising she wants to chase them.'

The Owl's other great love is the river Stinchar. At a shout of 'Walkkkk!' and 'Gumboot time!' all the dogs express delirious excitement. The Owl has been joined by her court: her granddaughter Memphis Minnie and

ABOVE: *Owlie avoids Mr Crocker's critical gaze.*

RIGHT: *Embedded in chintz.*

Dimmie, the Dandie Dinmont. River in sight, she races towards the water, grey hair flying in the wind, acolytes tumbling in her wake, all oblivious of the disapproval of Mr Crocket the fisherman. But she skids to a halt and settles under the umbrella of a huge gunnera leaf growing by the riverside. Mr Crocket, who has had a 'let rod', hiring the right to fish Bardrochat's stretch of the Stinchar, for the past twenty-five years, sucks on his pipe and looks infinitely relieved. 'There's a ten pound salmon over there by the far bank, but it might not be there for long.' Mr Crocket looks meaningfully at the Owl. Cecilia hastens to reassure her valued fishing tutor and river companion. 'Owlie loves to go in the river but she knows that she's not allowed to.'

The Boiled Owl is renowned for ruthless ways with the McEwen's friends and retainers. Alice, who had looked after the McEwen children for some seven years and been housekeeper for three, finally had her nerve broken by Owlie.

'We were coming back from shooting. In the back yard I saw Alice, frantic, wailing, with her hair all over her face. I thought something absolutely ghastly had happened – one of the children was dead, there'd been a car crash – but all she could say was that the dog had been gone for six hours. At which point, Owlie slunk out of hiding, absolutely thrilled with the success of her tease. I boxed Alice round the ears because she went completely hysterical and gave notice. "Out I am going," she said and out she went. So the poor Boiled Owl is known as a domestic wrecker.'

Hearing this tale, the indignant Owl retreats to Cecilia's lap, from where she can look down on her granddaughter with smug disapproval. Minnie was eating something that looked vile. 'Is it her bone? No, it isn't, it's the cat. Oh well, that's luck,' says Cecilia.

Ebony and Magnolia

MAJOR JOHN WILLS

LITTLEWOOD Flash, Meuse-Rhine-Ijssel bull, regarded himself lugubriously in the wing mirror of Major John Wills's car. He was to be dismissed. There was talk of his replacement because his virility had proved insufficient to ensure the future of his breed. At the ripe age of four, it seemed tough on a self-respecting bull.

His reflection in the wing mirror was impressive, reducing the car to dinky size and its occupants to nervous giggles. But, unconcerned by the mammoth in their midst, two slim black Labradors were mousing in the field. Their image appeared in the mirror and the bull's beady eyes snapped. Dogs are infinitely more interesting than cars, and the Herculean figure lumbered off to investigate. Unperturbed Ebony and Magnolia snuffled on, oblivious of discussions on pregnancy in short horn cows and various red and white Friesians. A mouse caught is swallowed whole, like an oyster.

Ebony and Magnolia (Nola for short) use the lake at Allanbay Park as their personal swimming pool. Once a pond, it was enlarged and landscaped by John and Jean Wills, then stocked with fish. It is now well worth a detour for Canadian geese, sometimes as many as 300 in a day. 'It's quite nice seeing them,' says John Wills a trifle doubtfully, 'but they do eat the most horrific amount of grass. It's hard to believe that three geese eat as much grass as a sheep or a cow.'

With the arrival of Ebony and Nola, the geese, ducks and fish disperse

ABOVE: *Stocked with fish, the lake has become a sanctuary for fish and geese.*

LEFT: *Ebony and Magnolia pose in front of their private swimming pool.*

125

so mother and daughter can splash, swim and retrieve sticks. The Labrador, also known as St John's dog, was once·an indispensable crew member of every Newfoundland fishing boat. British sportsmen turned the retrievers of fish into retrievers of game. The Earl of Malmesbury bought his dogs from Newfoundlanders delivering their fish to a British port in 1870. He always called the dogs Labradors and the name stuck. The Labrador has become well established in its adopted country and it is still Britain's favourite gun dog.

John Wills is tolerant of Ebony's and Nola's water sports. 'Good water dogs are an advantage for picking up the birds after the guns.' Major Wills does not shoot any more but, with his two dogs, he often joins the keepers to pick up stray birds and runners after the drives on a shooting day. Ebony is not quite sure about this; while happy to find the birds, she is not very keen on retrieving them in her mouth, unlike Nola who will retrieve anything.

Ebony and Nola have their annual holidays in Scotland. Every August the Willses, two-legged and four-legged, pack themselves into the car for the long drive north. Halfway house is the Auchen Castle Hotel, selected entirely for its five-star attitude to dogs. 'They allow Ebony and Nola in the house and there are the best walks ever in the garden. The're even kind enough to have a lake to make the dogs feel totally at home, so we always have to go there because it suits the dogs so well,' says Major Wills. 'Once they get to Scotland they adore it, marvellous smells and everything. Fishing is a bit tricky as Nola is absolutely impossible. Stalking is very hard work, as you have to keep the dogs low while crawling along the ground yourself. I'm thinking of designing camouflage coats for Labradors. Their black bodies do show up on the hill.'

Back at home the dogs have a strict regime. Up at 7.30 am, one Bonio after their masters' breakfast, then an aesthetic fast until tea-time. Ebony and Nola are treated to a different tinned food each day so that their palates do not become jaded, and the Willses have extra helpings of vegetables cooked specially for the dogs. They have a coloured bath towel on their bed which is changed once a fortnight.

But this highly organised life is not foolproof. Ebony was less than a year old when attacked on her own premises at Allanbay Park by the farmer's dog from next door. Fortunately he was a pedigree Labrador so, although the worst had happened (despite John Wills's effort to separate the runaway couple with a hose), Nola was the happy result. 'The puppies were all terribly nice but she was special,' recalls Major Wills, who was not pleased when the farmer claimed stud fees for his dog's marauding activities. 'His dog had come and raped my dog, in my garden, and he claimed stud fees. It seemed rather cheeky. I suspect he was probably sitting in the bushes waiting for it to happen. I offered him one of the six puppies but he refused.' Neighbourly relations are strained.

Determined Ebony should not be violated again, John Wills decided she had to be spayed. The date chosen was 4 May and the operation had been organised when the vet received a frantic telephone call from Major Wills lamenting that it was Ebony's birthday and he could not possibly allow the operation to go ahead. 'We've been labelled as completely dotty by the vet's surgery ever since.'

BELOW: *John Wills' dressing room doubles as the dogs' bedroom; the bathtowels on their beds are changed once a fortnight.*

Nelson

MR JACK PEACH

NELSON is a venerable sea dog. His home is a converted railway carriage on Winchelsea beach, and his life is spent supervising his master Jack's fishing nets in Rye harbour. They used to go to sea together, sharing the tiny wheelhouse perched like a telephone box on the rolling deck, but in old age they are content to let others gather the harvest of the English Channel, the whiting, cod, sole, plaice and dab caught in nets mended by Jack.

Jack Peach was a session drummer. A set of his drums fill his and Nelson's bedroom in the former guard's van on the shingle of the sea shore. He played in variety theatre in Manchester. After the war, he toured Britain and the Continent with a band, followed by a stint on the Queen Mary, criss-crossing the Atlantic between Southampton and New York. He returned to London after a few years to become a session musician for the BBC and various recording companies, backing Eartha Kitt and other top recording artists of the day. About eighteen years ago he and his wife sold their house in London in order to rent the railway carriage and buy a fishing boat. Life had come full circle from the Queen Mary. 'There is something rather romantic about a railway carriage on a beach,' he says.

Nelson was the result of a night on the tiles by a local mongrel and a Hungarian Vizsla hunting dog. His eight siblings were all put down, but Nelson was reprieved because of his rich, red colouring. He has all the

ABOVE: *A venerable sea dog.*

RIGHT: *The fishing fleet gone, Nelson and Jack enjoy retirement on dry land.*

attributes of the Vizsla, a breed dating back to A D 1000, combined with a certain mongrel cunning. Vizslas are robust, noble dogs with tremendous energy and cannot be confined, so Nelson was ideally suited to life as a beachcomber. As a puppy he was an indefatigable retriever. 'All the fishermen round here used to throw him the round rubbers that they put on the nets, and he'd catch them and bring them back. If you didn't throw it, he'd stamp on your foot,' says Jack. The dog lives off the fish brought in on the trawlers. 'He has a splendid appetite. The only fish I eat are dabs, haddock and small baby sole but he eats anything of any age – the older it is the better he likes it. The more revolting the better.'

In the days when Jack and Nelson were fishing themselves it meant twelve hours at sea, six days a week, but now aged sixty-eight and sixteen, they are happier on dry land. Jack sews the nets which, by law, in the Rye area have to measure a minimum of 75 millimetres. He splices the wires and renews the twine. 'I have no yearning to go back to sea again,' he says. Nelson is enjoying his retirement, seeing the fleet off each day on the high tide. The pair can always be found, regardless of the weather, near the trawlers at Rye harbour.

Jack Peach and Nelson at home outside their railway carriage.

Lucy and Totty

MRS RUPERT HAMBRO

'IF you have ever slept with a snoring peke, a man sounds really good,' says Robin Hambro, the elegant blonde wife of banker Rupert Hambro and owner of Lucy, a tiny black sleeve Pekinese. Stentorian snoring is hard to imagine from one so small. Lucy's head is no larger than a Cox's apple, but her character is enormous and the product of centuries of superior breeding for superior purposes.

The sleeve Pekinese is thought to be a miniature version of the Chinese Foo dogs who were distinguished by their leonine features and thought to ward off evil spirits. The Pekinese is said to have existed for 1500 years and the breed was the exclusive property of the Chinese Imperial Court. They were kept inside the palace walls to preserve the purity of their bloodlines and a staff of eunuchs was employed to nurture them. The emperors had portraits of the dogs painted in books to create a pictorial standard of the breed.

Seventh century Chinese chronicles record how Pekinese rode on cushions placed in front of the mounted emperor; the miniature dogs were venerated to such an extent that commoners had to bow to them and theft of a Pekinese was punishable by death. Cherished and honoured within the royal circle, the dogs were sacrificed on the death of their masters in order to protect them in the afterlife.

In 1860 British soldiers captured Peking and sacked the Summer Palace. The royal dogs were considered too precious to fall into enemy hands and

ABOVE: *Totty for once holds supremacy over the furious Lucy.*

LEFT: *Chalk House, an original posting house for the stagecoaches rattling between London and Oxford.*

so were slain by the imperial guard; only five survived, pets of a princess who had taken her own life but spared theirs. These dogs were brought back to England as trophies of war. The Duchess of Wellington and the Duchess of Richmond received two each and the fifth was presented to Queen Victoria, who named her prize Looty.

Those five dogs, together with later specimens imported from China, were the foundation stock of all Pekinese in Britain today. The breed's romantic origins, allied to Queen Victoria's approval, ensured instant popularity. By 1910, the Pekinese's dignity, loyalty and stubborn courage had made them the most popular toy breed in the Western world.

Lucy has all the attributes of her distinguished forebears, although her entrance into the Hambro family only came to pass through a small advertisement in *The Times*. It was, however, large enough to divert American-born Robin on a rainy English day when she was supposed to be enjoying some hearty shooting. Instead, she went to see the litter of Pekinese and fell in love with Lucy, the runt of the litter, unwanted because she was too small for breeding. Nevertheless, she had a determined nature and a devil-may-care attitude to life.

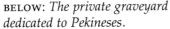

LEFT: *Elegant in a sea of Colefax and Fowler.*

Her country home is Chalk House in Berkshire, originally a posting house for the stagecoaches rattling between London and Oxford. When Lucy arrives after the vicissitudes of a hard week in the capital, she first satisfies herself that everything is in order. Then she disappears to torment her master's two Labradors in their outdoor kennel. 'She has to establish her superiority,' says Robin. 'Even in the black of night, she goes and stands outside the kennel and yap, yap, yaps. She then returns satisfied in the knowledge that she is in control.'

Lucy has one fellow house dog, a good natured West Highland terrier called Totty who struggles gamely to come to terms with the fact that she is decidedly second best in the eyes of everyone except her owner, Flora, daughter of the house. Since Totty's lineage only stretches back to Harrods' pet department, Lucy considers her beneath contempt. But Lucy herself is not quite perfect. An operation on her back deprived her of her breed's decorative mane. As if to compensate, she is particularly proud of the white gloves on her forepaws. Whereas less rarefied dogs sit up and beg, Lucy prays or claps with her pretty white paws.

The exotic history of the Pekinese blends well with Lucy's environment. Chalk House is described by Sir Nikolaus Pevsner in *The Buildings of England* as 'eccentric early Georgian . . . "Piano nobile" of five bays over a basement, the central doorway approached by a flight of steps. Hipped roof and high parapet curving down either side to eaves level . . . in the parapet four false painted windows and a central *oeil de boeuf*.' It has been singled out as one of 'the Lesser Houses' of Great Britain by a writer in *Country Life*.

Sadly, the town of Reading is now reaching out towards Chalk House, encroaching upon its privacy, threatening the peace of the graveyard at the bottom of the garden. This is no ordinary graveyard, but one dedicated to Pekinese. Headstones inscribed with the names Mrs Wiggs, Lotus, King, Coco, Tiddles and Tweed (another lone West Highland) stand in line. At the end is a tiny unmarked grave, a sad tribute to Moley, a peke that was a wedding present to Rupert and Robin Hambro. 'She was the love of our lives, but we couldn't find anyone to do a gravestone for her,' says Robin. Lotus and departed friends belonged to Lady Stair, the previous owner of Chalk House. It was a happy coincidence that the Hambros were brand loyal.

Lucy's predecessor, Moley, led a charmed life. Diving under a London taxi, she emerged unscathed on the other side. She also survived a night lost in London. While Rupert Hambro was searching hopelessly in Holland Park, Moley found refuge with a builder's draughtsman in Kensington High Street. Rupert was devoted to Moley but does not enjoy quite the same relationship with Lucy, who associates him with a lot of loud noise. Lucy is a one-woman dog, happiest with Robin. She is a decorative little dog who regards her black, fluffy self as an indispensable ornament to the Queen Anne house.

BELOW: *The private graveyard dedicated to Pekineses.*

Humphrey

MRS DAVID METCALFE

SILVER candlesticks glint in the flickering light; bejewelled ladies flash dazzling smiles at impeccably suitable men. Their varnished nails finger delicate glasses of wine as they exchange tantalising gossip in heavy Chinese whispers.

A superb shrimp soup is succeeded by a rich *boeuf bourguignon*. One lady wrestles with the impenetrable caramelised top of a *crème bruleé* while, at the same time, attempting to captivate her host, David Metcalfe.

Impossible as it may seem, one person is bored. Humphrey has endured more dinner parties than most cairn terriers and his ragged grey hair does nothing to hide his glum expression as he lurks discontentedly under the sideboard. He is banned from the kitchen during these hours and no-one is talking to him.

As far as he is concerned, the only interesting aspect of any party is the arrival of Henry the butler. In a ritual perfected by Humphrey over years, he waits at the top of the stairs – dishevelled head stuck through the bannisters – for the arrival of the black-coated figure. On seeing Henry go into the drawing room, the dog surreptitiously dives under a plump sofa to follow the butler's progress at ankle level.

Henry's routine is exact: he goes to the bar in one corner of the drawing room, carefully places the champagne glasses on a silver salver, then begins the return journey with his precarious load. This is Humphrey's moment. The canine torpedo fires himself from the sofa's skirts to sink his

ABOVE: *Humphrey and Sally leave for the office.*

RIGHT: *Humphrey hibernates among the hand-made shoes.*

teeth into a pin-striped leg. A satisfactory howl of pain is extracted, but the glasses merely shiver in firm professional hands.

Cairn terriers were originally employed by Scottish chieftains some five centuries ago to hunt vermin in the cairns, piles of stones which mark burial grounds in the Highlands. So fierce was the terriers' determination that they would even confront wildcats. James V, son of Mary, Queen of Scots, valued the dogs so highly that he sent six cairn-like terriers to the King of France around 1600. The precious cargo was divided into two groups of three and loaded on to two separate ships as an insurance policy against disaster at sea.

Sally plucked Humphrey from obscurity and took him to the rarefied confines of Belgravia. When, chic and elegant, she swept into the pet shop and demanded to buy him, the shopkeeper tried to persuade her to have one of the pretty puppies in the litter of cairns. But Mrs Metcalfe had made her choice: the thuggish individual who stood foursquare in the centre of his relations. 'He was just like a walking box. They did everything to dissuade me but I was adamant.' She returned home with the square box tucked firmly under her arm.

The next obstacle was Sally's husband. David Metcalfe looks like a cross between a Great Dane and a borzoi with a keen, enquiring nose. Immaculate in a blue suit, silk shirt and hand-made shoes, he nervously dabbed his enquiring nose with a paisley silk handkerchief and condemned the very idea of a dog with horror. 'It's cruel to have a dog in London, cruel to the dog, cruel to me and cruel to everybody.' So Humphrey had to be concealed in the cellar for four days. On the fifth he made his entrance. A

ABOVE: *Ensconced on David's cashmere knee, Humphrey can be confident that indignity will always be outside his experience.*

formal introduction between dog and master was effected and David Metcalfe's worst suspicions confirmed. Humphrey was everything he was not: shaggy, tousled grey hair on a round body, the tail a mere apology for a pipe cleaner. The first thing he did was spend a penny in the drawing room.

Now they breakfast together each morning. Bacon and eggs for two and a manly perusal of the *Financial Times* before Humphrey takes David to the nearest lamp-post. While David is in the City, Humphrey hibernates among his shoes.

The eighteenth century terraced house that is Humphrey's home was formerly owned by relations of Syrie Maugham who transformed the rooms into a world of mirrors and paintwork in white and shades of grey. Sadly the glass was destroyed before David and Sally came to live there. Sally, who is the London connection of an interior decorating business in Locust Valley, Long Island, has recently completed a number of rooms specially designed for her six-foot-seven husband. The chest of drawers is so tall that the average person is unable to see over the top into the mirror. Old cartoons by Dighton festoon the walls in the bathroom where a giant bottle of bath oil, specially recommended for infant bathing, dwarfs a collection of ivory. A bear, suitably named Humphrey Beargart, sits complete with mackintosh and felt trilby on David's bed. The walls are covered in Norwich paisley shawls. Orderly rows of astonishingly long, hand-made shoes sit in the cupboard beloved by Humphrey. He roosts here, grubby, grey face contrasting oddly with the immaculate cashmere suits and crocodile belts arranged above him. From his hiding place he enjoys an exclusive view of a watercolour portrait of his master which leans against the wall on the floor. It shows David, depicted as a giraffe, in shooting clothes complete with gun and two black Labradors.

Humphrey has most fun in the drawing room. Quite apart from butler-baiting, he has perfected the art of pulling the blinds behind the curtains. On hearing the click of the blinds, when they are raised, Humphrey instantly appears from the farthest corners of the house with a view to a kill. By launching himself at the pull cord, he can lower the blind and, once down, give it a savage shaking. This game is repeated nightly. A fascinated crowd has been known to gather in the street outside to see Humphrey's undercarriage in full flight halfway up the window, the blind clamped in his teeth and his little legs flailing against the glass.

At one time the blind game may not have been sufficient to satisfy Humphrey's macho instincts, for he became very aggressive towards other dogs, particularly if they were on leads. So much so that Sally Metcalfe consulted Mr Phido, a dog psychiatrist whose visiting card portrays a dog reclining on a *chaise longue*. Mr Phido claims to have cured a fierce dachshund who reduced its owner's visitors to creeping round the house behind a protective fireguard. Sally Metcalfe was most impressed by this recommendation. 'He suggested the way to cure Humphrey would be a two-hour session in our house with everybody who was close to him. I was desperate to do it, with a tape recorder hidden under the table, but David refused.'

After their initial differences the boys are now sticking firmly together. Entrenched on David Metcalfe's navy cashmere-clad knee, Humphrey can be confident that such indignities will always be outside his experience.

BELOW: *A fascinated crowd has been known to gather in the street below to see Humphrey's daily trick of chasing the blind up the drawing room window.*

Rosie Abel Smith.

Beaufort

Mrs Robert Abel Smith

THE mountain of presents under the Christmas tree shivered, tumbled and fell. Out of the avalanche emerged Beaufort, a wire-haired dachshund complete with red ribbon who toddled over to Rosie Abel Smith. 'I held him in the palm of my hand and that was that,' says Rosie. From that moment, seven years ago, the dog and the artist have been inseparable.

Rosie paints dogs in watercolour and Beaufort has acted as her mentor and critic. He is no oil painting himself, looking like a cross between a moth-eaten loo brush and a Swiss roll, but he has been remarkably generous in his unqualified approval of Rosie's portraits of other dashing young dogs. Beaufort can be very voluble when he wishes; if he is asked a question at meal-times which he considers sufficiently pertinent, he will sit up, put his forepaws on the table and sing.

Beaufort has his own special chair at the table in the kitchen of their house. Rosie's husband, Robert, says: 'I can never have romantic dinners with Rosie alone. There are three things I hate about dogs – bad breath, yapping and licking – and Beaufort is guilty of all of them.' Beaufort is well aware that he is not Robert's favourite person. Every night when Robert attempts to get into bed beside his wife, the dachshund stands foursquare on her tummy baring his teeth. 'Then he makes the most unbelievable noise, a sort of demented squealing, when Robert picks him up,' says Rosie, with a giggle.

The Abel Smiths' house has a view of the source of the Thames. It looks

ABOVE: *A commissioned painting by Rosie of Beaufort.*
RIGHT: *The voyeur at a romantic dinner for two.*

straight out over the shallow dip where a tiny bubble of spring water gurgles from under one little stone. Beaufort often has a refreshing drink at the beginning of Britain's greatest river. It is also a house with a secret. 'It's a crooked house. It used to be thatched and the thatch reached right down to the ivy. But then everything was ripped off and it's now a nude, Victorian monstrosity. I think the architect must have murdered his wife because there's a mystery room in the middle. Nobody has ever found a way into it because the walls are too thick and quite blank. Either it's a tomb or he was such a rotten architect he got his plans wrong and had too much wall,' says Rosie.

Her summer studio is the garden which suits Beaufort ideally. Having settled Rosie at her easel, he will retire to sleep in the spinach leaves. Rosie had no formal artistic training – 'I went to cookery school, not art college' – but she used to paint birthday and Christmas cards for her parents and loved painting for fun. It was when she moved to Gloucester-shire that she decided to give up cooking for a living and try something else. 'I thought the country was all about hunting and having animals and, as I'm completely animal-mad, I started painting pigs.' They sold well. Rosie also started dealing in English watercolours. A special commission for a friend inadvertently began her dog portraits. 'I take in every detail when I meet the dog but work off a roll of film for composition.'

Beaufort features in a whole series of her pictures which has made him rather a pin-up and quite restored his confidence after the arrival of Toby, Robert's flat-coated retriever, and Bodge, a waspish terrier. Beaufort's hair fell out because he resented Bodge so much. But then he acquired a fan club of people who demanded pictures of him sitting bolt upright at table, or toying with a piece of cheese on his plate, even full frontal. As this all required Rosie's undivided attention, the dachshund's rapid decline halted. Toby and Bodge are relegated firmly to the kitchen floor while Beaufort, in his chair, conducts his own particular brand of sparkling conversation at meals in little barks and trilling growls.

The garden studio. Jealous models jostle for position.

144   BELLA, WENDY, SHEILA, SPOT AND REX

Bella, Wendy, Sheila, Spot and Rex

Mr Jimmy Nairn

JIMMY Nairn is gamekeeper to the Duke of Roxburghe, in charge of 5000 acres of pheasant shooting, two grouse moors, seven spaniels and two Labradors. He masterminds fifty days' shooting every year for the 'guns', guests who mostly pay for the privilege of sharing Guy Roxburghe's sport. Jimmy organises the 'drives', when the birds are driven towards the guns by the beaters, and agonises annually about the state of the grouse moors where adverse weather conditions or disease can be the ruin of the most challenging shooting in the world. Grouse cannot, yet, be artificially reared, although Jimmy rears 6000 pheasants in pens beside his cottage, Floors Kennels. His sons and his dogs are his assistants in his job. Both Ian and James Nairn are also gamekeepers on the Roxburghe estate; the dogs are the field workers, an integral part of the shooting scene in which man and his best friends work together for the sport and pleasure.

Visit Jimmy at home in his stone cottage and, like a cauldron boiling over, the spaniels spill off the sofa, vying for the attention of their master comfortable in his chair by the coal fire. For contrary to the practice of many keepers, Jimmy brings up his dogs in the house. His home is their pre-prep school for service in the field and on the moor. 'The puppies get their confidence from being with you,' he says. 'They need contact in the

RIGHT: *Jimmy Nairn and Rex.*

LEFT: *Like a cauldron boiling over, the spaniels fight for position in front of the fire.*

145

same way as a mother and baby, so they sleep in the house for six months before going out to the kennel – if I can persuade the wife.'

Primrose Nairn nurtures the future shooting stars with her husband. 'The dogs cling to her when they're young. She feeds them and walks them, but when they start working they're finished with her.' It is a man's world out with the guns.

The spaniels have to be self-sufficient. 'A dog is no good to me if it cannot find me. I do not look for the dog. When I'm at a shoot my responsibility is to look after the guns, and I'm never far away from the Duke. If anything happens I have to be there. So at the end of a drive it's no good if my dog is lost. Many times the dog has to find me; many times I have to stick to His Grace, and if I decide to jump in a Land Rover my dog has got to be there with me to jump in too. I cannot go looking for it.'

Jimmy Nairn's current team includes cocker spaniels Bella, Wendy, Sheila, Spot and Rex and Labradors Tina and Betty. At one time he kept only Labradors but now favours the cockers because he thinks they have more character.

Yet Bella, thirteen-year-old matriarch of the family (Spot and Wendy are her son and daughter, Sheila her granddaughter), seemed a very weak character at first. She originally belonged to the late Elizabeth Roxburghe, widow of the ninth Duke, who married Jocelyn Hambro and who wanted a dog with which to pick up the birds after a drive. But Bella returned from her training in England gun-shy and was given to Mrs Nairn as a present. 'She was an outcast,' recalls Jimmy. 'If they're not working dogs I have no time for them, and whenever I took Bella out she ran straight home at the sight of a gun. So we decided to have puppies from her for her own good.'

Jimmy and his four-legged family at home.

So Spot was born and taught his mum new tricks. 'He started to work very, very quickly and, one day when we were going out to grouse, I said to Bella, who was sitting on a chair, "Do you want to come then?" and she came out on the grouse moor all day and has never looked back. I think the young one conveyed to her what a grand time there was to be had.'

Bella still valiantly goes out despite an accident three years ago. Crossing the road to rejoin her master at the end of a day's shooting, the spaniel went straight under the wheels of a Land Rover. 'I thought that was the end, so I picked her up and took her away as I thought she was a goner,' says Jimmy. 'Then she started to pant so I laid her gently at the side of the burn and sprinkled water on her face. The Duke came down and asked, 'Is she gone?' and I said, 'No, she's coming round,' and she did. The front wheel had run right over her back and the next day she was very, very sore and could not move. I had to lift her everywhere, but a fortnight later she was out again. It was unbelievable. I think she'd rolled with the Land Rover.'

Wendy has also had a narrow escape. 'We were out picking up ducks one morning and there was one duck in the middle of the lake which I sent Wendy to retrieve. But its wing stuck right over her eyes and she started to swim round and round and round, without knowing where she was going. She became so tired she sank, still holding the duck. I shouted to my son James, 'Wendy is going to die, I'm going in,' and started to peel my coat off, but James never hesitated, he ran straight in and when he reached Wendy she was going down for the second time, still with the duck. When James pulled her out I had to stand and hold her until all the water ran out of her mouth and she recovered consciousness. But she was never going to let go of that duck.'

Spot is the best of Bella's family and a natural choice for Jimmy. He has a penchant for spots. His ferrets all have spots on the tops of their heads. When Mrs Nairn viewed Bella's first litter she knew immediately which puppy would be chosen. She was right; her husband returned with the liver-and-white bundle in his arms, with the definite spot on the top of its head. A formal introduction was made. 'This,' said Jimmy, 'is Spot.'

Rex is the new baby and the new strain of spaniel in the Nairn home. He came from the Duke of Westminster, the Duchess of Roxburghe's brother, and at the age of four months started Jimmy's special form of training: retrieving his master's cap. The skills of a gamekeeper's dog include finding 'runners' or wounded birds, and retrieving them to their master undamaged in their soft, spaniel mouths. Stealth is clearly going to be one of his strengths as he has perfected an SAS-style crawl towards the cottage fire. Now he will enjoy his first season with the other four dogs, learning from Bella's wisdom, Wendy's perseverance and the natural abilities of Spot and Sheila.

He will be encouraged with kindness. 'You get a lot of things with kindness,' says Jimmy, who carries out the ultimate kindness himself: he puts his own dogs down when they are too old, sick or injured. The dogs are his companions through every working day, helpmates and friends, devoted but disciplined; Jimmy has to rely on these right-hand lieutenants. 'A dog that lets you down is no good to anybody.'

Kelly

Mrs Jake Morley

KELLY is a mongrel who was once raffled for 50 pence in a pub. Today she can hold her own with the best shooting dogs in Yorkshire. Yet when Davina Sheffield first met Kelly, she was a cringing, bony, black bundle attached by a piece of string to the desperate teenager trying to sell her.

'I was in a pet shop in Kensington,' recalls Davina, 'and they were explaining to the young girl that they didn't take dogs and that she should leave the puppy at Battersea Dogs Home. I'd always thought, wrongly, that Battersea destroyed unclaimed dogs at the end of a week and no-one would have wanted Kelly, she looked so disgusting. Then the girl told me how her father had won the puppy with a 50 pence ticket in a pub raffle, but her mother was allergic to dogs and the girl had twenty-four hours to rid the family of the unwanted prize. I took her telephone number and promised I would arrange something.'

Some weeks earlier Davina and her sister, Laura Pilkington, had decided they needed a dog for their house in Oxfordshire. A yellow Labrador had been their initial choice; a moth-eaten mongrel was what they actually got. Davina collected Kelly from a London tube station. The puppy matured to look very similar to a black Labrador, only with a white shirt front and a stumpy six-inch tail. Well-fed and cared for, she thrived on life in London during the week and in Oxfordshire at weekends.

Then Davina married Jake Morley and Kelly began another new life in the Yorkshire dales. Now home is a farmhouse sheltering beneath moors

RIGHT: *Kelly's favourite position on a grouse butt.*

LEFT: *Kelly and Tom awaiting elevenses in the kitchen basket.*

ABOVE: *Kelly and a neighbour amongst the Toile de Jouy.*

that climb to 1400 feet above sea level, where merlins, golden and green plover, curlew, dunlin and snow buntings can be found. Woodcock nest down the dale by the house, and coveys of partridge take dust baths under the cars in the drive.

But Kelly specialises in grouse. Shortly after his old Labrador died, Jake Morley took Kelly shooting for the first time at one of the finest grouse moors in England. Davina says, 'I thought he was joking and she'd run a mile, I was panic-stricken all day. I knew there'd be really smart dogs there.' But at the end of Kelly's first day out Jake judged her 'the shooting dog of the year' and has taken her with him ever since. 'Grouse are her forte,' says Davina. 'She'll find any dead grouse for miles around. She

ABOVE: *Merlin, the unwelcome rival.*

BELOW: *Davina and Kelly on the hill above Westerdale.*

watches intently during the drive and marks exactly where the birds fall. I have to hang on to her, otherwise she is off like a rocket.' At the beginning of the day's shooting Kelly may accompany Davina with the beaters, walking towards the line of guns driving the birds forward, and, when the drive is over, picking up the grouse. 'She brings the birds back oven-ready, especially runners which are quite dead by the time Kelly has retrieved them. It infuriates the other pickers-up.' The Morley world centres round their moors; some shooting days are let during the season and there is work to be done throughout the year, burning the heather, gritting and keeping the bracken at bay.

Kelly is also a fisherdog. She has enthusiastically plunged into the river Spey after Jake and Davina but she is encouraged to rabbit on the bank, returning frequently to check on her owners' progress. 'She won't go in a river if it's dangerous; she can smell a depth. I think that's the whole point of a mongrel, they have so many different talents,' says Davina.

Kelly has now acquired a companion, Merlin, a yellow Labrador. 'Kelly cried when Merlin arrived,' says Davina. 'In fact she cried for three months, until Merlin was old enough to play with her on the hill.' The puppy has reduced Kelly's bedroom in the cloakroom to a sea of torn newspaper.

The farmhouse in Westerdale is isolated, often cut off by snow in the winter. High above on the hill are two crosses where sweethearts Ralph and Betty braved a snowstorm to meet but were lost in the blizzard and died within 200 yards of each other. On the north side of the dale three stones mark the spot where a mother and her two children perished in a snowdrift. Kelly has inspected these memorials on many walks and, when it snows, she sensibly retires indoors to lie inside the huge open fire-place. Davina believes it is a reaction to her sad start in life. 'I'm sure she was frozen as a puppy and starved. She eats like a maniac, as if she remembers what it was like to have nothing.'

Matthew, Mollie and Jasper

MR AND MRS JOHN NUTTING

MATTHEW is a top dog. His breeding is impeccable, his home one of the finest early eighteenth century houses in England. Matthew was decidedly meant for Chicheley Hall.

The Scottish terrier was not for sale when Diane Nutting arrived at the kennels to buy a Scottie puppy from breeder Muriel Owen. Before she left home Diane said to her husband, Johnny, 'If I get a dog I'm going to call it Matthew,' yet none of the puppies appealed. 'I wandered round the pens and found this bigger dog sitting all alone and went back to Mrs Owen and said, "That's the one".' But as the son and grandson of champions, the dog was being kept for breeding; Diane Nutting was only able to take him after paying a small fortune and promising to show him and permit stud duties. As she left, Mrs Owen called after her, 'We've even named him, we've called him Matthew.'

So the Scottie, descendant of Gaywyn Kingson and Gaywyn Top Hat, arrived at Chicheley in Buckinghamshire where Georgian craftsmen had executed some of their best work and the resident ghost is supposed to be a dog. A portrait of this ethereal spaniel hangs in the breakfast room. It is supposed to scratch on the door, although no-one, least of all Matthew, admits to a sighting.

Chicheley Hall was built for Sir John Chester between 1719 and 1723. Some 955,550 bricks were used in the construction of the house, wings and garden. Indeed Chicheley is distinguished by some of the finest

ABOVE: *Matthew and Mollie Nutting contemplating their position.*

RIGHT: *Diana and Matthew exercising in front of Chicheley.*

brickwork in any house of this date. The front door is modelled on an engraving of Bernini's Chapel of the Holy Crucifix in the Vatican, the garden door taken from a plate of Borromini's Oratory of S. Filippo Neri. The windows on the main front copy a doorway of one of Rainaldi's palaces, and those on either side of the front door are modelled on Soria's St Catharine of Siena. So Chicheley boasts inspiration from four of the leading architects of baroque Rome.

Matthew doubtless appreciates these fine points because he becomes very grumpy during the winter when the family retires to the old stable wing while the main house is spring-cleaned. The Scottie is thus deprived of his favourite refuge on a window sill in the panelled sitting room. Here he can avoid the attentions of Jasper, John Nutting's exuberant flat-coated retriever, who kisses everyone indiscriminately, man or dog. The window sill is preferable, even though Matthew is there forced into rather closer proximity with his wife, Mollie, than he really likes. Matthew and Mollie do not have a deep and meaningful relationship. Her presence at Chicheley was tolerated solely to produce a son and heir, which she has failed to do. It is an irritating reflection of Matthew's prowess at stud, and he cheerfully discards his wife in favour of regular visits to Mrs Owen for more fruitful purposes.

Matthew and Mollie share the window seat without speaking to each other. He is haughty, his heavy eyebrows and bristling moustache resembling those of a distinguished army colonel, honed to perfection in the days of the Raj. It is said that when the Romans invaded Britain the Scottie was already a well-established terrier in the Highlands. So it is understandable that Matthew despairs of Jasper's lack of *gravitas*. 'He is a constant embarrassment to me,' says Johnny Nutting. 'The first day I took him out shooting was in Essex and I think he ended up in Norfolk. On the second outing in Northampton, he ended up in Gloucestershire. He's really not interested, just tremendously enthusiastic so every available bird is sniffed, picked up, and dropped before he tears off to the next one. He has never been anywhere smart, we are not asked to shoots where any manners are required. He retrieves everybody else's pheasants but fortunately fails to bring them to me which would inflate my score beyond belief.' Flat-coated retrievers are said to be more outgoing than golden retrievers and Labradors. They were originally Newfoundland dogs, brought to the British ports by Canadian seamen. Collie and setter blood was introduced to the breed which had become quite rare until a flat-coated retriever was chosen as Cruft's champion in 1980.

Matthew considers Jasper altogether too undignified for Chicheley. The retriever has a habit of slithering breakneck across the cool marble hall, an unfortunate contrast with the Palladian style which emphasises correctness and restraint. The main door-case is a model of sober classicism, and on the chimneypiece is the stately lion which was put on the table facing the German commander at the surrender of the German fleet in 1918. HMS *Lion* was Admiral Beatty's flagship, and the naval hero's collections are housed at Chicheley.

In 1952 the Admiral's son, the second Earl Beatty, bought Chicheley Hall from Sir John Chester's descendants. Lord Beatty died fourteen years ago and his widow, Diane, later married John Nutting, a distinguished barrister. Chicheley, although imposingly grand, is very much a

Johnny and Jasper, his constant embarrassment.

home and the family – Nicholas Beatty, to whom the house belongs, his sister Miranda and half-sister and brother Victoria and James – live in all of it. No apartments are roped off from the public, so that they can see tapestry designs after Goya (the originals of which hang in the Prado in Madrid) as well as The Quorn at Hoby Vale by Lionel Edwards, painted for Johnny's grandfather Sir Harold Nutting, Bart, Master of Foxhounds. Lord Beatty's study contains the naval desk used by the Admiral on HMS *Lion* at the Battle of Jutland. It was designed to be used while standing. Some of his many decorations hang on the walls, including the Grand Cordon of the Excellent Crop of China.

Matthew rejoices when Chicheley is reopened to the public each Easter. Then spring-cleaning is over, the main staircase (for which a craftsman was paid three pounds, nine shillings for '9 dozen and 7 Bannesters and 5 columns' in 1723) no longer a skating rink of polish. Matthew is ever present in the public tea room to share buttered scones and crumpets with his guests. He can be king of his particular castle again.

Symphony in blue.

Blob

❖

MRS ROBERT DUCAS

FIRST-TIME visitors to the Clock House in Kent are warned, 'Do not leave your car on arrival. Do not for any reason open the car door.' This is for welcome guests. A large notice in the courtyard informs the un-welcome, 'Burglars Beware. Approach with Care. Dangerous Dog.'

There are dangerous dogs who, put to the test, roll over and have their tummies tickled by burglars, and there are Dangerous Dogs. Suffice it to say that Blob, a German pointer, has sent twelve people to hospital, although none required stitches. The postman was pinned to the ground and sat upon by the enthusiastic liver-and-white hunter. Yet his owner Patricia Ducas insists Blob was perfectly adorable as a puppy.

The visitor, marooned in his car behind closed doors, has to be released by Dudley, former groom to Patricia Ducas's string of Russian horses, and now butler and dog-minder. He locks Blob in the kitchen before admitting guests through the front door. Once admittance has been gained, the dog and the visitor are formally introduced, whereupon Blob adopts the pose of congenial host. Butter, it seems, would not melt between his ample German jaws.

He stalks guests to the drawing room which was converted from a large garage block that once housed a fleet of Rolls-Royces. The floor slopes towards the drain in the centre of the room, a relic of bygone car washing. Blob's favourite place is a huge sofa above the drain, now covered by an elegant Russian carpet, it is a suitable vantage point from which to spot

LEFT: *Once inside the drawing room of the Clock House, Blob adopts the pose of congenial host.*

ABOVE: *A beach on the Kent coast. Patricia and Blob relax after a morning at the fish market.*

the approach of offending cars through the window. 'He's a fantastic guard dog, casual callers seldom come here at all now,' says Patricia Ducas.

She has taken certain precautions for anyone who does brave the Clock House. 'Blob has destroyed an awful lot of clothes, hence all the track suits upstairs. If somebody has their clothes ripped from their body, I can quickly rush them into a track suit.' Fortunately Blob is none too accurate. 'He's getting so quick and is dying to bite someone so much that he misses them in the headlong rush.'

German pointers are one of the best all-purpose hunting dogs, skilled at tracking their quarry by day or night. Bred in Germany in the seventeenth century by crossing Spanish pointers with bloodhounds, the dogs were prized by both noblemen and poachers. During the last century breeders added English pointer blood to improve the strain's running style and poor scenting ability. 'He doesn't smell at all, so when he rushes over to me in the garden, I'm not absolutely sure if he knows it's me, whether he's going to grab me by the throat or is just pleased to see me.'

Blob is very talented at getting out of places – 'He eats his way out of every single door at the Clock House, chewing round the frames until he can escape' – and he is equally gifted at getting into things. He once broke into a sealed basket of special tins and lobsters, that were sitting on the back seat of Patricia's brand-new car – 'The result was horrendous, bright red shells strewn throughout the car, and the smell of fish growing stronger by the moment.' The happy hound, with no sense of smell, sat in the centre of the debris, totally satisfied with his morning's work. Luckily success had not been total; despite the many teeth-marks, the valuable tins remained intact. Not even this dog's outstanding destructive talents can open a tin of caviar.